GARY BURGHOFF:
TO M*A*S*H AND BACK

My Life in Poems and Songs

(THAT NOBODY EVER WANTED TO PUBLISH!)

BY GARY BURGHOFF

GARY BURGHOFF:
To M*A*S*H and Back
My Life in Poems and Songs
(That Nobody Ever Wanted to Publish!)
©2009 Gary Burghoff

Published in the USA by:

BearManor Media
P.O. Box 71426
Albany, Georgia 31708
www.BearManorMedia.com

ISBN-10: 1-59393-343-6 (alk. paper)

Edited by Lon Davis

Book design and layout by Valerie Thompson

TABLE OF CONTENTS

◌

To My Brother David who remained
Faithful through the wounds
Which "Fame" inflicted.

To my three children
Gena, Miles and Jordan
For raising me right.

To the M*A*S*H cast and crew
Who fought for excellence always.

And to the Creator for the
Life contained within.

FOREWORD

☙

The big trick will be to keep this from becoming a fan letter.

The hell with it — I'll just go ahead and gush.

Gary Burghoff may be about the best actor I've ever worked with. Why?

Maybe it's because he possesses a talent as large as his heart, a heart whose size is enough to make even the great outdoors seem slightly claustrophobic. In my (not so really) humble opinion, what makes Gary the standout performer he is is the fact that his dramatic skills, skills that have been fueled by years of training and experience, have been honed by the trials and tests of real life which have shaped the man within.

Whatever the reasons, Gary brings a laser-like commitment to the roles he chooses, combining that dedication with a personal and professional standard that considers one hundred percent merely a starting point.

As an actor, he has the uncanny ability, one that is given to only a chosen few of those who ply the same craft: the added gift of enhancing a writer's work, of adding breadth and depth to his or her creation, of breathing life into words in ways that are as unique as they are surprising. For those of you who enjoy cherries on top, by employing his special form of acting alchemy, Gary is able to slip inside the skin of any role he portrays in a way that makes him seem to *inhabit* a character instead of merely enacting one.

Exhibit A; He has an uncommon way of making a funny line even funnier, of enhancing a poignant moment by making it all the more so. And whatever it is that he contributes to a bit of dialogue or mood of a scene is never once at the expense of however many other players he might be sharing the screen or the stage with.

With this book, Gary Burghoff puts his make-up and his wardrobe aside and Gary Burghoff, the author, makes his entrance and gives us a glimpse of what the far less public side, the off-stage, off-camera side of Gary Burghoff is all about.

What follows is a self-portrait of the human being, the face without the artifice; the husband and the father; the protector and the kindred spirit of every other species with whom we share this fragile planet; the Gary Burghoff that is ever-ready to act as their protector, their ombudsman and, through his most impressive painting skills, their Boswell.

Having raised five children, I've become an old hand at paternal feelings. That is how I have always felt about Gary. Protective. Possessive. Concerned. Not that he's not perfectly capable of fending off an enemy (some of whom have turned out to be himself), but I find some comfort in thinking that I'm always there to offer him as much of that commodity as I can.

The best kind of son a father (or even a father figure) can hope to have is the kind who grows up to become your friend — and that is what Gary Burghoff surely has done.

So much for prologue. There is a life waiting to be told in the pages ahead.

I won't keep you — or Gary — waiting one word longer.

LARRY GELBART
SEPTEMBER 2008

Weep onward child of poet's song,
Pasteled in hues of bluish void.
Weep onward child of Poe and Freud,
And dream your dream of sorrow.

The news is bad again today,
The papers sweet with deadly truth.
Weep onward child of twisted youth,
And more will come tomorrow.

— POEM BY GARY BURGHOFF
©1967

CHAPTER 1

⌘

It was 1949. I was having the dream again. It was as if I were a living camera, looking out through my own lens. I viewed a quiet meadow, green with new spring grass. The sky was calm, clear, and very blue. At the bottom of a knoll, the lush green grass formed a bowl, filled with placid, clear ground water. It was always the same. I awoke, and felt euphoric. The feeling lasted for several minutes until I shook off sleep and began another day of life in my sixth year.

My father, mother, brother and I lived in a small Victorian home in the town of Forestville, Connecticut. I shared an upstairs bedroom with my brother David, who was six years older. Our two-story house was white with green shutters, much like all the homes on East Main Street, homes filled with normal, peaceful, average, dysfunctional middle-class American families. Dysfunctional? You bet, though we had no idea we were. Who knew? By whose standards did we judge ourselves? Sigmund Freud was long since dead and "therapy" was not a word in our vocabularies. Neither were words such as compassion, tolerance, sensitivity, ecology, under-standing, and duality. That was all somehow functioning in our lives, but the words were never used, nor our neuroses identified.

The two words I did hear often were *love* and *progress*. If a week went by without my mother quoting a Methodist sermon entitled "God is Love," or dad dismissing destruction of our natural environment with the phrase "that's progress," my six-year-old mind would have been very confused. Those two words encompassed all I needed to know. If God is love, I was expected (having been cre-ated in His image) to be lovable and to love others. And, I was expected to overlook the destruction of natural beauty in the name of progress. Hmm! How simple! Too simple, I was to learn.

These were exciting times although I had no way of knowing it. Just four years earlier, we had won World War II. Everyone was rebuilding! A new concept had arisen in American home construction called *tract housing*. That meant a small network of streets lined with identical little homes, one blue, another white, then yellow, otherwise all the same, thirty feet apart, on very small lots. No room for vegetable gardens, chickens, goats, a family cow, horses, trees . . . just manicured green lawns and a one-car garage. This was new to us, and although we never owned a cow, some of our neighbors did, along with chickens, ducks, and goats. People still brewed dandelion wine in sheds. Some even had outhouses!

On weekends, I would be driven a few miles to the Rhineflesh Farm to spend two eagerly awaited days doing chores, riding the ponies, and plucking freshly killed chickens for dinner. Although the killing was, at my request, not one of my duties, I accepted it as the normal way of things. Evidently, "God is Love" did not extend to chickens! I remember feeling a mild sense of guilt because I *did love* chickens, and found the conflict between loving them alive and loving how they tasted discomforting.

One evening at the dinner table, at our house, I refused to chew my food.

"Gary, what on earth is the matter?" my mother asked.

"I'm trying not to crush the germs," was my answer.

"What germs?" asked Dad.

"The germs we can't see. They live on everything, especially food. I read it in a book."

"Here! Eat this part. Germs don't live on this part of the chicken."

Paranoia set in as my brother David sneered. My dad was offering me the ass end of the chicken. I knew what it was. I had plucked it! My feelings were hurt, but I believed him. I had seen what came out of that end. No self-respecting germ would occupy that part. To this day I only eat dark meat.

I know it now, but had no idea growing up, that my mother and father had formed an unholy agreement regarding our upbringing. I mentioned Freud earlier. Although his contribution in uncovering the secrets of the Id was not spoken of in our everyday lives, his concepts lingered in the contemporary literature of the time. My mother followed the permissiveness of Dr. Spock while my father was true to his Methodist instruction of "spare the rod, spoil the child." By the time I came along there had been so much disagreement concerning the raising of my brother, they had decided to *split* the responsibility of parenting their two sons. Dad would raise Dave; mom would raise me — each according to their individual and opposing parental philosophies. Talk about duality!

I hope new parents are reading this. Be united in raising your children! Consistency matters. Our parents' decision had the effect of causing the worst kind of dissention between my brother and me. We were always competing: I for Dad's attention, Dave for Mother's. And when that attention was not forthcoming, we became, all too often, jealous and resentful of each other.

I remember endless hours shared between my dad and brother, designing and building a boxcar in the cellar in anticipation of David's entry into the annual Soapbox Derby. Meanwhile, Mom delighted in my imitations of Bette Davis and Jimmy Durante in the living room, and while I was grateful for her attention, I was wishing for a boxcar of my own under Dad's instruction. For all I knew, Dave was wishing he could be imitating Bette Davis in exchange for Mom's approval!

Before marrying Dad, Mother's name was Ann Rich. She never knew her father. To this day I don't know my biological grandfather's first name! "Mr." Rich deserted my maternal grandmother in 1914 when Mother was only two years old. I know little of the relationship between my grandmother and Mr. Rich. Only one story from a great aunt comes to mind. My aunt answered the telephone, soon after Mr. Rich's departure. The voice asked for Anna, my grandmother. My aunt handed her the phone. My grandmother heard one word from Mr. Rich and fainted, spread-eagled on the floor, out cold. He probably had only said, "Anna, it's me." That's all it took to send Grandma into unconscious oblivion. Pretty powerful relationship there, I suspect.

My mother had two brothers, my uncles Joe and Freddy Rich. They all lived with my great-grandparents, the Carpenter family who were first generation Italian-Americans. In addition to my great-grandfather Gioacchino, who was a tailor, there were Great-

Grandma Carmella, great uncles Fred, Spartacus, Eddie, Rebell, Dewey and Great Aunt Adelaide. Add my grandmother with *her* three children and you had a house full!

At some point, my mother at age two was given, for a few years, to the next-door neighbors to be raised by a woman named Nellie. In all my years growing up, I had never seen a picture of my maternal grandmother, yet Nellie's photo had always graced my mother's bedside nightstand. The story goes that, after years of Mom's bonding with Nellie, my grandmother suddenly reclaimed her daughter! Not much was ever said about the trauma caused by the occurrence. The impression is that it was abrupt, deeply painful, and produced lasting neurosis, which will be discussed in following pages. I will say now, that it is unequivocal in my hindsight that Mom was "crazy."

Her paranoia, emotional outbursts, attention deficit disorder (not clinically recognized at the time), caused much pain, confusion, and uproar throughout our entire family as Dave and I were growing up. But she was also kind, compassionate, very intelligent, generous, charming and talented. And, in her own flawed and confusing way, she was loyal and completely dedicated to her children. In other words, Mom was a woman you sometimes hated to love. But love her we did. Duality.

I remember the nighttime arguments emanating from my parent's bedroom. "These kids think more of their dog than they do of me!"

"Boys always love their dogs. It doesn't mean they don't love you."

"See! You never support me! Now you're taking the dog's side! It's that mean streak that runs through your family!"

WHAM! I don't know what hit the wall, but it did so with such ferocity that I ran naked to hide in the shower! When Dad found me I was practicing "duck and cover," an exercise taught at school in a futile attempt to survive an "atom bomb" attack. Dad asked, "Gary, what are you doing?"

"I was afraid. Did you and Mommy hurt each other?"

"No! Everything's all right now. Go to bed."

Go to bed? No talking about it? No explaining what had made the walls shake? Maybe going to bed made sense. Maybe I'd have the dream again; then things might *really* feel "all right." But try to sleep in total darkness after the bomb! Total darkness? Dad insisted on it. To him, an active imagination was to be discouraged, and mine had been activated! They had just *tried to kill* each other! Suddenly it was completely silent and dark, and everything was supposed to be "all right." I was only six, but somehow *all right* didn't fit.

I lay there for what seemed a decade. Finally, I yelled, "Da—aad!" I could hear his slippered feet shuffling down the hall . . . on clicked the light from the wall switch.

"What's the matter?"

"Can I please have the light on?"

"No! There's nothing to be afraid of. See?" Off went the light, then on again. "Everything is exactly the same in the dark as it is when the lights on." Off went the light.

My jaw dropped! It drops today when I recall his flawed reasoning. Everything was the same in the room, but everything had changed in me. I was terrified. There were things they weren't telling me: reasons why they argued, dark corners to their relationship that erupted suddenly and — to my six-year-old perception — violently. Could *I* have caused any of the trouble? *Go to bed, with the lights off? Was I being punished? What else weren't they telling me? Maybe monsters* did *exist.* Suddenly, I was, for the first time, afraid of the dark! It took endless hours to fall asleep. The dream didn't come.

In the morning after my parents went downstairs to prepare breakfast, I crept silently into their bedroom. Amazingly, everything was in total order! No blood on the walls, no shattered furniture. Even Nellie's photo was unmoved. And later, over bacon and eggs, Mom displayed no bruises. Everything was normal. Everything except my trust and confidence. I would fear the dark for many years to come.

My father's name was Louis Rodney Burghoff, but everyone called him Rod. It's a man's name, and my father was perceived by most as a "man's man." He was quintessentially athletic, tall and handsome. He fished, hunted, had a masculine sense of humor, treated others in a gentlemanly fashion, and for a time went to church on Sundays.

Dad was born in 1910 to Louis and Eliza Burghoff, my paternal grandfather (a first-generation German-American) and my grandmother (who was English). Grandpa Burghoff's brother married my grandmother's sister. Thus, the Pierce sisters became Eliza and Emily Burghoff, nearly overnight spawning a huge Burghoff clan. In my father's home there was my dad, my uncles Lesley and David, aunts Phyllis, Doris, and Rosemary, also known affectionately as "Pokey." In Great Aunt Emily's and Uncle Oscar's family lived cousins Chet, King, and Margie. By the time I was born in 1943, when you combined both sides of my family I had cousins in every corner of Connecticut.

There was great energy and stability on the Burghoff side of the family. Before we moved to Forestville from the neighboring town of Bristol, my grandparents had lived just across the street. I can remember them well. There was much laughter in their house and warmth. My grandmother's hugs were nearly overwhelming, and her kisses very wet, but her humor was engaging, and she enjoyed my brother and me. *She was glad we were born.* There was no question in our minds.

One day I'd dress up as a cowboy and shoot all the imaginary "bad guys" in her backyard.

"Gary, I hope you don't kill all the bad guys today! Grandma called. You'll need some for your next fantasy."

A few days later I'd show up in my tight pajamas with a red towel hanging down my back.

"Who are you today, Gary?"

"I'm Superman and I can kill just the same!"

Not very funny I admit, but she laughed and laughed and told that story all her life.

Glad we were born? That to me is the essence of good parenting. No matter what you do or what you say to your children or grandchildren; no matter how you struggle or how disappointed you may be at any moment with them, always respond in a way that says *I'm glad you were born.* It's the difference between saying "what's the matter with you?!" and "I don't understand what you were thinking when you put the cat in the washing machine. Go to your room till you can explain it." The first response declares "you are *hopeless!*" The latter encourages self discovery and responsibility.

Grandma Burghoff always stressed the positive. She was the easy one to love.

In the summer, we would pile into my father's Lincoln and drive twenty miles to Harwington, Connecticut, where we owned a small lake-front cottage. My grandparents owned a cottage nearby. I remember joyful evening hours of card games, iced tea, cookies and laughter with all the Burghoffs gathered around the dining table. This was family. We were close, and we enjoyed each other. I was a very lucky little boy. I was living the great American dream and life was (on the surface at least) good.

One night, I removed a curtain rod from my bedroom window, borrowed some sewing thread and a safety pin from which I fashioned a fishing pole. I went outside, caught a worm on the wet grass, attached it to the open safety pin and flipped it into the lake. To my amazement, I caught a fish almost immediately! Hearing my screams of excitement, all the family came running out, into the night, to share my jubilation. Why I remember this little occurrence so clearly, even today, some fifty-eight years later, attests to how important small early achievements can be in our lives, with family supporting and sharing the experience.

The summers at Lake Harwington were heaven. My dad taught me to swim and at least once took me fishing. As we trolled the large red and white striped Daredevil lure around the edge of the lake, we noticed our neighbor Mr. Johnson feverishly casting off his dock in the distance. A half hour later we passed right in front of him. *BAM!* That's where I got my strike.

"Pretend there's nothing on your line," Dad whispered.

"But, Dad, it's really heavy!"

"I know, but for God's sake, just hold him until we get passed Mr. Johnson. You've just hooked *his* fish!"

So, as we both tried to stifle our laughter, I pretended that nothing really unusual was happening, smiled and waved at Mr. Johnson as we passed, and as soon as we had rowed around the bend, *I reeled like hell!*

With Dad cheering me on, I landed my first big fish, a twenty-four inch pickerel. That was the fish the "big boys" caught, and my dad had shown me how. That was a good day. It was the closest I would ever feel to my father.

With children, it's the *little things* that count. It's taking time to help them catch a fish, a parent's ability to put aside the adult frustrations of the world and just be with your kid, even if it's just for a few minutes every day. That's the way to say "I'm glad you were born." It's building a model airplane together, enjoying that rainbow or colorful sunset. It's *capturing time* together, often without words.

My father was very critical. He had a low tolerance for "failure." If I mistakenly inserted the model airplane wing in backwards his disapproval was immediate. I had no time to discover my mistake. It was "Oh for God's sake, look what you're doing! You're not following the instructions! *What's the matter with you?*" The last part was rhetorical. It implied there was something "wrong" with me. Looking back I was internalizing the negative.

I had been born with a deformed left hand. Before I write another word, I must make a firm assertion. There is only one kind of 'handicap." It is the disposition of your mind. If you perceive yourself as disabled . . . you are! Otherwise your "deformity" is no more an impediment to your life than are the differences in individual's noses or earlobes. We are all "normal," except those of us who mentally buy into abnormality. Regretfully, at six, I was buying in.

I had been learning that my parent's words could be deceptive. Words such as "special," "above average," "exceptional," were often used to describe me. But, their attitudes nullified their words. I was aware of my mother's guilt feelings over having borne a "deformed" child and while my father handled it more casually, I sensed their alertness to the possibility that my physical difference was only the outward sign of other internal disorders.

Once while I rode in the back seat of the family car, I asked my dad and mom a question about the law.

"Dad, if you're lowering a piano on a rope, from an upstairs window, and the rope breaks, and the piano falls on top of your best friend, is that murder?"

Other parents may have viewed such a hypothetical question from a six-year-old as, at worst, precocious. My parents seemed shocked and speechless! To my humiliation my mother silently mouthed the words "a criminal mind," in my father's direction.

Now you must understand that, at this point in time, one of the biggest hits on Broadway was a play called *The Bad Seed*. It was a play that put forth the idea that, criminal rehabilitation efforts aside, some people are genetically born criminals. The play had become a main topic of conversation among mother's social group, and (like me) she had a very active imagination. But, why did she, in my case, imagine the *worst?* She could have just as well mouthed: "He's going to be a lawyer!" (At the time, an unquestionably respected profession) — Or at least . . . "a piano mover."

Dad reacted with annoyance; not so much at my question as to mother's negative conclusion. Nonetheless, I had the feeling that I had caused his annoyance.

I would have to learn to curb my curiosity around my parents.

"A TREE"

A tree has its roots in the ground.
So it never goes walking around.
It just grows towards the light
But when day turns to night
It's gained hardly an inch or a pound!

Now we people are much more dynamic.
In a car, a jet plane, or a hammock.
We scurry about
With much worry and doubt.
Our ambitious exploits panoramic!

Human conquests and wars are historic,
Though few of us feel quite euphoric
We yearn to be healthy
Respected and wealthy
And often take much Paregoric!

Now I've seen all of life I can see.
And one prospect is troubling me.
I've achieved all I can.
By the values of man
But I find that invariably

The god who made earth, sky and sea
Probably sees me as a flea!
And though I'm no ignoramus
And to men I'm quite famous
I will ne'er stand tall as a tree!

— EXTENDED LIMERICK BY GARY BURGHOFF
©1996

CHAPTER 2

❧

You wouldn't know it if you saw it today, but in 1949, my home at 78 East Main Street was a little boy's paradise. It stood on an acre and a half, adorned with giant oak trees, which sheltered a huge grass lawn that seemed to extend gracefully and endlessly toward a distant brook and pine forest. There were fish in the brook, along with frogs, colorful water snakes, turtles, and wild water plants. One of them, known as "skunk cabbage," fascinated me. If you tore off a leaf it would emit an odor so repugnant that even a self-respecting skunk would immediately flee the area.

I would spend endless hours in the forest, often encountering rabbits, squirrels, opossum, an array of songbirds, pheasants and grouse, butterflies, raccoons, and sometimes deer. On one occasion, while following a narrow deer trail, I encountered a most beautiful red fox. He showed no fear of me. We just stood there calmly gazing at each other eye-to-eye, more in fascination than apprehension. He was even calm enough to sit only a few yards before me, our eyes still engaged.

To me, it was an experience akin to my dream. I felt peaceful and calm. Many years later, I would become an oil painter. One of my first paintings would be called "Eye To Eye," and it would be of that fox, his eyes searching my soul for unspoken questions only our hearts could answer. All that seemed disjointed and confusing at home became unimportant and tolerable when I was in the woods. This was where *REAL* was. *Here*, life made sense.

Twenty years later in New York City, James Tuttle, my acting teacher, would calm my frustration over not being able to master an acting exercise by quoting the poet, saying, "A crooked tree is only searching for the sun." It would be a breakthrough moment for me. I knew what the poet was saying. I had been to the woods.

It is the crooked tree which has the most character. It is the one struggling to grow in the shadow of the more powerful. It is he who has to work harder to find the light, and once found, change direction, if need be, to reach the sun. There is dignity in the struggle, and there is a greater dignity when you finally reach the sun, that no one can ever take from you. James Tuttle and the poet would encourage, but nature was my inspiration.

I am constantly amazed at the arrogance of mankind. We worship our scientists, inventors, artists, industrialists, engineers, developers, chemists and explorers. Yet, we sadly fail to recognize that all great discoveries are *borrowed* from nature. Even the greatest abstract painter borrows color, form and texture from the environment. Great paintings are not created. They are *remembered*, whether the artist is aware of it or not. And no famous explorer ever discovered a great land that wasn't already *there* through the process of nature. In a very real way it is nature which discovers us. Its bounty and beauty lures us, beckons to us, and draws us out, to find it. *Nature motivates mankind.* We owe it everything, and while it generously gives us all we need, it owes us nothing.

Whenever I see a clear-cut forest, or a construction crew indiscriminately bulldozing trees to clear a lot, it is difficult to contain my frustration. Trees are our loyal, silent, partners; living symbols of struggle and triumph over adversity. They are the living equivalent to the Washington Monument, and every bit as important to our heritage and identity.

Am I sounding pompous? Consider this: When God gave us "dominion over nature," was he granting permission to destroy his creation? Or directing us to *nurture* it? It is a far more pompous attitude which disregards a tree's right to exist or the rights of other creatures to their habitat.

My youngest son Jordan (who, among other professions, aspires to be an architect) one day offered a solution to habitat encroachment: "You know, Dad, we should be building a lot more homes underground. Then the environment would be allowed to continue unmolested."

What an interesting solution. He didn't mean that we would become a society of "mole people." With modern technology and fiber optic lighting, an underground home would include large video screens, which could reveal the unspoiled natural surface environment as brightly as any modern picture window. They would be safe from hurricanes and tornadoes. Energy costs would go down due to the fact that the earth's crust maintains a constant 55 degrees. Add a few non-intrusive solar panels at ground level and many of us would be selling energy to our power plants. Meanwhile, on the surface, the world would continue to become a paradise and that is something *it is thoroughly resolved to do.*

I believe in the concept that our world is a single living organism which has been set in motion to, through competition of its individual parts, achieve an ultimate state of perfect harmony and order; in short, PARADISE.

You need only to stop and look for proof of this theory. Ever see a blade of grass forcing its way through asphalt? It is proclaiming its intention! The world intends to become a paradise!

While we often see chaotic, weed-choked fields and cramped forests, we are viewing only a short-term part of the unfolding process. When the early settlers came to the new world they witnessed immense forest systems which had been undisturbed by mankind for thousands of years. They marveled at the perfectly ordered stands of giant oak, ash, maple and pine, which had evolved into an ecosystem, the majesty of which they had never seen! It was a system of beauty and order, which supported an abundance of life unparalleled in human imagination! Then, out of ignorance, instead of drawing from the abundance, they proceeded to destroy that majestic canopy (which had supported the abundance) in order to create fields on which to grow their crops. In doing so, they were gaining the farm . . . but losing *paradise.*

The instinct which fires my passion concerning the environment was not learned. I was born with it. In 1949, I performed my first (and only) "criminal act." While passing Mr. Geaudot's family farm on my walk to Greenhills School, I noticed that his "imprisoned geese" had no water. My immediate neighbors, the Swanson family, had a goldfish pond. I kidnapped poor Mr. Geaudot's geese and deposited them into the Swansons' fish pond.

It took several trips to pull it off. Imagine a six-year-old toting seven fully grown, honking, biting, uncooperative, geese two city blocks toward a more natural destination. This was no covert act. I'm sure the whole neighborhood was alarmed at the clamor. But before they could identify the source of the sudden turmoil, I had completed the objective. Mrs. Swanson came out of her kitchen to view, with amazement, seven happy and very large water fowl, romping playfully in her six-foot pond! Within minutes, Mr. Geaudot arrived to retrieve his geese, my parents had been phoned, Dad's leather strap had been removed from its hanging place by our back door, and I spent the rest of the day in my room trying not to sit, while the sting receded from my backside.

Next to our house, we had a big red barn, the first story of which had been converted to a two-car garage. In the rear of the garage was a small room which I converted into what I referred to as, "the little museum." Outside on the street, I placed a sign that read "Little Museum . . . 10 cents," which included an arrow pointing toward the garage. It was a child's version of the Museum of Natural History, which we had visited in New York City, the only difference being that my museum contained no taxidermy. Everything walked, slithered, crawled, exuded slime, and chirped within that six-by-eight foot room. Shelves lined with jars and cages contained a wide array of living creatures from bugs to field mice. No one to my recollection ever paid the price of admission, and all the specimens were eventually released, but the benefits of hours of observation, studying their behavior, and how they interrelated, far outweighed the disappointment of my first failed enterprise.

જ   જ   ⌘   ⌘   ⌘

My mother was a dancer. Before she met dad, she had been well known in the Bristol-Hartford area, as one of the best dancers and dance teachers. She had studied with the famous Anna Pavlova in New York, and appeared in vaudeville. She had dreamed of a career and if you could have seen her, as I did, you would have known she could have rivaled the best dancers in America. When I was born, I had to be delivered by C-Section. From that time, she was plagued by poor circulation in her legs, causing sudden and painful muscle cramping, making a career impossible for her. Her creative aspiration took other forms. In addition to teaching dance in Bristol, she wrote poetry, scripts and songs for musical productions, and directed local theater.

I was attending rehearsals for her local charity reviews and musicals as far back as I could remember. And though I was considered too young to participate, the stage life experience was definitely luring me. In the late '40s and early '50s, Bristol spawned some very talented people. Tap dancers, singers, and musicians of the highest order, combined with less talented members of our town, to create original musical productions of such positive energy, color and gaiety that local audiences flocked by the thousands to our auditoriums.

Bristol was, at its heart, an industrial town; a center for the manufacture of clocks, ball bearings, brass components, and fishing equipment. Nearly everyone had a good job and, as with all successful industrial communities which flourish, there was generosity. Our citizens financially supported a multitude of charities and community projects: boys' clubs, girls' clubs, summer camps, fundraisers for the United Way, war bonds, etc. The town was vibrant with activity and civic pride. My father was foreman of the Engrham Clock Company and founded the Forestville Boys' Club.

Each year our local boys' club would create a vaudeville-style production to be performed at our local high school auditorium, which sat an audience of over a thousand. My mother broke tradition one year by writing and directing her own musical, complete with story line, original music, and choreography. Our house was alive with actors, piano players, conductors and stage hands during the pre-rehearsal preparation. I was enthralled with their enthusiasm and the pure fun of it.

One afternoon when they had left for the day, I went into the front room where Mother kept her musical compositions and phonograph. I found a record entitled "I'm a Lonely Little Petunia in an Onion Patch." I played it while lip- syncing the words. Mom heard the music and investigated. Though I had no idea she was watching from behind the half-closed doors, she was doubled over with laughter at my antics. As the record ended, I saw her.

"Play it again," she said. "I'll give you some tips. You're very funny."

From that moment, I was in SHOW BIZ!

Within a week I was performing at rest homes, clambakes, and fundraisers for the "mentally challenged." My act was comprised of impersonations of famous movie stars and . . .

I'm a lonely little petunia
In an onion patch.
An onion patch.
An onion patch.
I'm a lonely little petunia
In an onion patch.
And all I do is cry all day!

At one country clambake, I performed atop a picnic table with many of the local farmers (wearing their Levi coveralls) as my audience. They threw genuine silver dollars on the table as I performed! *I was a hit! Now I was being paid!*

I remember thinking, "HOLLYWOOD HERE I COME!" — and I was serious.

One autumn afternoon, I wrapped a peanut butter and banana sandwich in a bandanna, tied it to a stick (no kidding), slung it over my shoulder and ran away from home. Destination: Hollywood! I walked about five miles to the nearby town of Plainville, got tired and crawled into a large sewer pipe at a roadside construction site. My short nap was interrupted by the kind voice of my Uncle Fran (Great Aunt Adelaide's husband) calling from his oil delivery truck. He had spotted me while passing by. Actually, he and just about everyone else in town were out looking for me — even the local police force joined the search; their chief was another uncle, Dewey Carpenter. Mom of course was frantic when she discovered the note I had left on the kitchen table:

DON'T TAKE THIS PERSANELL,
IV RUN AWAY TO HOLLYWOOD.
LUV, GARY.

After three hours of agony, and having alarmed the entire community of Forestville, Mom, in desperation, was about to phone the FBI, when Uncle Fran deposited me at the front door.

"Ann," he said, "I found him! I told him that Hollywood was in the other direction. If he continued the way he was going he would have ended up in the Long Island Sound! Maybe he should go back home and study the atlas."

The only studying I did was in the art of the strap; this time from both parents and three days of solitary confinement in my room. Hollywood would have to wait.

It was just as well, winter was on its way and that meant Christmas. For months I had been saving pennies. Smiling relatives on visits would give me one, I'd search for them on sidewalks, or horde them from lunch money. I even found one in the urinal in the Cameo Movie Theater bathroom. (I may have left that one.) In five months I had five hundred saved in a jar I kept hidden under my bed. They were saved to buy a Christmas present for my mother.

When no one was around I would count them, while fantasizing her delight upon opening the special present I would buy her with my own money. Even harder for me than the saving was the choosing. No matter where I went, my eyes searched for the perfect gift. Mom owned a small antique shop which she ran out of our front room. Her taste in antique glass was impeccable, her shelves adorned with peach-blow, Steuben and Tiffany. As Christmas approached, I had still not found the perfect gift. Anxiety was setting in. At appropriate moments (and some not so appropriate), I would urge my father to take me shopping on the sly, always careful not to let on to mom what we were doing. It had become a major project. After all, giving was, according to what I had been taught in a Methodist home, better than receiving. The Lord had said so. Through my project I was learning why. My projection of mother's appreciation and joy was strong impetus and this year it far overshadowed my expectation regarding the present Santa would bring for me.

Dad and I had nearly exhausted every available source. Finally, in one hardware store where we had stopped to buy lights for the tree, *I saw it!* Propped against a wooden stand on the top shelf, was the most beautiful plate I had ever seen. It was a decorative relief depiction of a 17th century Dutch artist painting, the portrait of a beautiful young woman. It had a shiny glaze, and looked *antiquey! Perfect!* I tried to contain my excitement. "Dad! Dad! Ask the man how much that plate costs!" It was $4.95. I was almost there! With tax, $5.15. My spirits collapsed. In a last-ditch effort, I promised Dad that I would continue saving the extra fifteen cents in exchange for a loan. He agreed! He wouldn't even charge me interest. *I had done it!* Now all that remained to be accomplished was choosing the finest wrapping paper, card and ribbon. I couldn't wait for Christmas morning.

Our parents had bought us "The Twelve Days Till' Christmas Calendar." It was hung on the wall in our room, brightly decorated with glitter, and contained small punch holes, each one representing a day in the Christmas countdown. When you punched out a hole, a Christmas scene would be depicted beneath; a picture of a candy cane, a child's tricycle, or a puppy with a ribbon bow around its neck.

The days passed so s-l-o-w-l-y.

By the time I had punched out December 19th, my body jiggled and jerked with anxiety. On Christmas Eve, I had trouble sleeping. All night long I would pull out the present from under my bed; each time examining the wrapping to be sure of its perfection, and projecting mother's look of surprise and joy upon opening it. When my Engrham windup alarm clock sounded at 6:30 a.m., I shot out of bed and, with present in hand, ran downstairs to the Christmas tree in the living room. Santa had been generous. Gifts were piled under, around and stacked high against the wall behind the tree. I was the first one down and I waited earnestly for Mom. The ten minutes it took for the family to stretch, shake off sleep, dress in robes and slippers, felt like hours for me. Finally, they descended. As Mom entered the room, I ran to her with my treasure.

"Oh . . . for me. How nice."

There was no enthusiasm in her voice. "Open it first, *please!*" I excitedly urged.

She sat on the Queen Anne upholstered chair, unceremoniously removed the wrapping, glanced at the contents and said glibly: "Oh, I don't like this sort of thing . . ."

Casually placing it aside, she rose and as she left the room, said coolly, "I have to make breakfast."

So much for better to give than to receive! *I was devastated!*

What was the reason for her passive cruelty? Had I done something to deserve her coldness? Had she and my father fought the night before? Did she just awaken in a state of depression? At six, my powers of reasoning were undeveloped. What made the humiliation much worse was the total absence of consolation from my father. He had observed the rejection. He had witnessed the saving, the planning and the months of earnest expectation. Yet there was no response. I was grieving.

For years to come, this single occurrence would shape the way I would view the world. Years of analysis, soul searching and self realization would reveal that all my inner demons could be traced directly back to that one traumatic moment, frozen in negative time and space, when my mother rejected my love for her.

There would be good times and bad to come. But I would shield myself against pain. I would fail in my school work or at any endeavor or achievement my parents wished for me! I had been thrown off track toward abnormality and I would be running away to Hollywood in my subconscious mind . . . *every* . . . *single* . . . *day.*

Whoever made the decision
To invent the television . . .
Should be shot!

— GARY BURGHOFF
2006

CHAPTER 3

CR

As 1950 rolled in and I opened the presents at my seventh birthday party, my favorite was a handmade radio from my brother David and my dad. The inner workings were from an old Motorola, but the cabinet was painstakingly crafted and decorated with powder-blue enamel and decals, complete with a shiny brass handle on top for portability. It was a heartfelt consolation that one of their projects in the cellar workshop was solely devoted to me. Dave and I kept it on the nightstand between the two beds in our room. Dad had eased up a bit regarding our bedtime schedule and we were allowed to stay up (lights on) 'till nine.

That radio! That wonderful magical box! It was a conduit to a world of laughter, learning and imagination unequaled in our lives. In this present age of visual imagery, it is difficult to explain to post-radio generations how special radio was to us.

My fear of the dark was obliterated by programs such as *Superman*! *The Shadow*! *Duffy's Tavern*! *Burns & Allen*! *Jack Benny*! *The Lone Ranger*! *The Bickersons*! *The Great Gildersleeve*! and *Fibber McGee and Molly*!

I was an ear-witness to the legendary live broadcast of *The Jack Benny Show* when Mel Blanc (the thief) placed a gun to Benny's back and (in a menacing tone) uttered, "Your money or your life."

Benny (the cheap skate): *no response.*

After the live studio audience laughed for one and a half minutes (a radio eternity) . . .

Blanc: I said your mon —

Benny: I'M THINKING IT OVER!!!

Another eternity of laughter from the audience and from all of us listening in.

My parents were listening the night Orson Welles nearly inspired mass suicide with his unbelievably realistic — or should I say *believably real* — dramatization of H.G. Wells' *The War of the Worlds*, which caused actual panic in American streets from coast to coast! We were unfazed at our house because we had listened from the beginning and heard the CBS announcer introduce the program: "And now, Orson Welles and the CBS Mercury Theatre Players present . . ." But those citizens nationwide who tuned in during the performance heard a documentary-style delivery from those excellent radio actors, so convincing that most thought they were listening to an actual emergency news broadcast, declaring that a Martian invasion was in progress, and they were destroying the world as we knew it!

That was the power of radio! It was an art form which not only respected but encouraged *active imagination*. It didn't entertain *at you*, it entertained *from you*! You had to mentally participate.

Often, I would fall asleep before the Lone Ranger and Tonto caught Black Bart, and on those nights I'd sometimes have my dream.

Radio was my Valium.

But in 1950, there was another box in town. It sat in the window of our local hardware store. In the evening, as we walked along the street, we would see a dim, flickering, greenish light emanating from that store front and reflecting on the mesmerized faces of our friends and neighbors who had gathered on the sidewalk to gaze at it. I can remember my father and me nudging our way through the crowd to grab a glimpse at the object of our neighbor's stupefied attention.

It was a radio with an EYE! A little grayish, green eye, about three inches wide, which was visually enlarged by a huge magnifying glass placed on a stand in front of it. I was standing to one side and could only see the pulsating light, but I heard a man's voice say: "This is John Cameron Swayze: Let's go hopscotching around the world for headlines!"

I looked up to see the slackened jaws of my fellow Forestvillians and nudged a little closer to the center. Then *my* jaw slackened! In the middle of the eye sat a little *man*! A talking, moving, *little man*. A little, talking, moving, John-Cameron-Swayze-Man, in the middle of a greenish, gray, eye!

"Dad," I whispered. "What kind of radio is it?"

"Television."

My world had changed *again!*

My father died in 1979. I was asked by my grieving family to remove his personal effects from his bedroom. Among them I found a small diary, in which only one entry had been made. It was in mother's hand writing.

"April 7th 1950. We never go out anymore. Television is now showing full-length motion pictures."

Not only did most Americans "never go out anymore," if mother was an average example, we stopped writing in diaries also.

Before television, Americans were *doers*. After, we became *watchers*. It was the beginning of the end of Big Band concerts on the green, roller-skating rinks, tobogganing with friends on snow-clad hillsides in winter, spontaneous neighborhood baseball games, full churches, doctors making housecalls, boys' and girls' clubs . . .

Recently, I reminisced with my two sons, Miles and Jordan, saying "You know, boys, I'm from the last generation who knows what life was like before television, computers, inside plumbing, air conditioning, washer/dryers, microwave ovens —"

Miles interrupted with: *"the wheel!"*

The laughter which ensued shut me up. But it's true. How did we survive before television? I am among the last who could answer that. We not only survived, we *flourished*. We flourished because our country was the extension of our states, our states the extension of our towns, and our towns the extension of our families. All of it, one giant, complex, wonderful, support system, of DOERS.

Television disrupted all of that!

Now we began to curtail doing things together, as a community, as a society. Instead of visiting Uncle Joe, we stayed home to watch "Uncle Miltie." Much of it was great entertainment, and sometimes even educational, but the world had lost an important part of its soul. Am I being radical? So be it. It's what I believe. But I didn't believe it in 1950! From the moment dad came through the door with our first TV — with its enormous sixteen inch screen — I was hooked!

After the tumultuous experience of figuring out how to attach the rabbit-ear antenna, there was that John-Cameron-Swayze-Man (only more life sized), reporting news from far-off places and bringing the world into our living room. We hung on his every word. It was as if Jesus was busy, and God had sent us a new messenger of truth! And we (especially mom), derived a form of marriage counseling, watching *I Love Lucy*. Somehow the Ricardos were working through our problems for us. All we had to do was *watch*.

I didn't have to go outside to shoot the "bad guys" anymore: Hopalong Cassidy was shooting them for me. I fantasized he would somehow call and ask me to be his sidekick, but he didn't. So I just sat there *watching*. Dave and I were learning to be perfect siblings, watching Ozzie and Harriet's David and Ricky, whose bland sense of humor was beyond our comprehension. Although the canned audience laughter was abundant, the words weren't funny. It was the droll delivery we were adopting.

"Hi, David."

"Hi, Gary. Where'd you get that terrific ugly shirt? Ha-ha . . . (snort) . . . ha-ha."

We were learning to master the funny putdown. And Dad would watch hours of baseball, football and basketball, reminiscing, instead of playing catch with us in the backyard.

It was a different sort of paradise; one you could watch unfold without physical or mental participation.

Now I may be overstating my case about TV, but you get the point. Years later, the final episode of *M*A*S*H* would nearly empty the streets of New York, the most active city in the world, as citizens retreated into their homes to WATCH. And that's an historic fact!

Through the 1950s it dominated every aspect of our daily lives. Students couldn't wait for the bell to ring, so they could run home, hurriedly finish their homework, and watch *The Mickey Mouse Club* or *Dick Clark's American Band Stand*. Our seventh grade teacher Mrs. Heffernan would play the piano "just like Liberace" had the night before, when she watched.

My favorites were the westerns: *Gunsmoke, Have Gun, Will Travel, Maverick, The Rifleman, Bounty Hunter* (with Steve McQueen), *Wyatt Earp*, and *Bat Masterson*. The program list of network westerns seemed endless, yet I could never get enough!

Dave and I were constantly searching the toy department at Muzzy's Department Store for the most realistic "six-gun" outfits. The stores were always out of "Fanner 50's," the one toy gun which in my mind most closely simulated the Colt Single Action Army used by virtually all the television cowboy actors.

Evidently, the adult male population was being affected also. Overnight, antique gun collectors sprang up everywhere, searching for all varieties of the famous Colt pistol. In 1950 a good specimen sold for $25. Today, up to $250,000!

David would later become a renowned collector of early and rare Smith & Wessons, with his national magazine articles and gun guild presentations, well known to hobbyists nationwide. I'm a collector of assorted American handguns from the Old West period of 1849 through 1910.

And TV was made to order for dysfunctional families! In the afternoon, the soap operas would dominate. Every negative human quality imaginable was now entering our living rooms! It was negatively cathartic. You felt almost better about yourselves knowing there were people who were more devious, manipulating, and had worse problems than your own. But, we were not conscious of its negative effects. We were in love with it. And I couldn't wait to someday be on it.

I had been held back in the third grade. My teachers at Green Hills Elementary were at a loss to explain to my parents why a boy so bright was "not applying himself." And I had become "disruptive" also. Actually, what I was doing was trying to entertain. I was attempting (inappropriately I fear), to introduce laughter into nearly every classroom experience. I was learning to master the *formula joke*.

"Boys and girls, who has ever heard of the poet Shelly?" the teacher would ask.

"I have! I have!" I would shout. "She's my favorite!"

"Shelly is a man," my teacher responded.

"Shelly Temple is a man? Boy, they got good makeup artists in Hollywood! *Who knew?*" I'd get a laugh, but my poor third grade teacher's curriculum was in shambles.

One day I asked if I could go to the bathroom. When I returned, at some point, I interrupted again. To my embarrassment, no one laughed.

"See — if you don't laugh at him, he'll stop!" said the teacher.

While I was away in the bathroom, my teacher had instructed my fellow students in the art of ignoring me. I felt betrayed! I thought I had been providing a service. Didn't everybody think that school was boring? I was just trying to lighten things up a little.

I know now that I was, on my terms, soliciting attention in rebellious defiance of what my parents or other parental figures expected of me. *If I had only paid more attention to picking the right moments, I might have been more successful. After all, comedy is timing!*

So I failed the third grade. My mother felt that rather than repeating it with the same thoroughly frazzled teacher, it would be better for all if I attend a different school. So they shipped me across town to Bristol's Clarence A. Bingham School. It had a reputation for its liberal yet disciplined environment. That reputation was well deserved. Most of the teachers there made learning almost interesting for me, which really began to screw up my comedy timing. Most of the time, I was actually listening to my instruction. These teachers were lousy straight men and women! All they wanted you to do was learn something, and some of them were funnier than I was! After awhile I couldn't stand the competition, and I began to shut up. My grades improved, but my rebellious nature had only gone dormant. By the time I had reached the seventh grade, my home life would take an ugly turn and *God Help Mrs. Heffernan!*

"I MADE IT"

Walter Pitkie was a genius,
And I wanted to be best.
So I copied from his paper,
And I handed in the test
For Mrs. Heffernan to grade it
And I made it!
And I wanted to play baseball,
But, I couldn't make the team.
So, my father bought the uniforms,
And mother kept 'em clean
To keep us happy when we played it.
And I made it!

When you're failing,
Keep on trying.
No one cares you'll
Soon be dying!
And I read that getting sterile
Was most definitely in.
So I wrote down where I'm going —
and I mentioned where I've been.
For Mrs. Heffernan to grade it
And I made it!

— SONG LYRIC BY GARY BURGHOFF

©1965

CHAPTER 4

CR

In 1955 my father was promoted to Vice-President in charge of manufacturing of the Engrham Clock Company. To my mother, this necessitated a move to a bigger house in a more "prestigious" neighborhood. It meant leaving the perfectly good home we loved, but to Mom, keeping up appearances outweighed just about everything. There was a question as to whether Dad could afford a new home, but in the end, the enthusiasm over his promotion threw caution out our old Victorian window.

My uncle Spartacus (Spark), who was Bristol's most successful developer, was summoned, an architect hired, a lot on prestigious Dewitt Drive chosen, and we were on our way back to Bristol. When the house was finally completed, it was (for me) like moving into a fantasy home. It was a huge, sprawling, three-bedroom, three-bath ranch, where everyone had plenty of "private space." My room contained my own private bath, and was designed to surround me with aquariums full of colorful tropical fish from every corner of the world. David's room was clear at the other end of the house. We hardly ever saw each other — I was lucky to bump into him on the way to the kitchen. Mom and Dad's room had a separate office adjoining it, and a large master bath. Then there was the formal dining room (which we never dined in), and the enormous living room (which we never lived in), and the "TV room," which was our true living area, where we spent most of our time together, if we chose to be together. We also had several telephone extensions.

One day, when mom and I were home alone, the phone rang. We answered simultaneously, she in her bedroom, I in the kitchen. I heard a man's voice:

"Mrs. Burghoff?"

"Yes?"

"We have followed up on the information you gave us, and haven't found any evidence of Mr. Burghoff's infidelity."

I was listening to a private detective! My mother had hired him to investigate my father.

"Mrs. Burghoff, are you there?"

"Uhhh . . . yes . . . yes, I am."

"I see . . . you can't talk now. Is that it?"

She knew I was listening.

"Yes . . . yes, I'm sorry." *Click. Buzzzzzzz.*

Amid a flood of surging emotions, I was flabbergasted. My dad cheating on my mother? To this day, I don't believe he was. My father, though at this point exasperated with mom over his feeling of having been manipulated into building a new house, loved her nonetheless. There was never a question in anyone's mind as to his integrity and loyalty to his family until now.

I was never told the details, but there was a woman who at one time worked at my father's factory, and who had called several of the executives' wives with individual claims of wild encounters between their husbands and other women. After wreaking havoc with several families, the woman was found to be a mentally imbalanced liar. I choose to believe, even today, that that was the case with my dad. You must remember this was 1957. Infidelity was not only grounds for divorce; in some places it was considered a serious crime. My dad, however, had moral and religious convictions. But the arguments ensued soon thereafter, and they grew in intensity and one night, as it did years earlier, something hit the wall so hard that one of my aquariums sloshed water over onto the carpet in my room! And that's when my seventh grade teacher, Mrs. Heffernan began encountering the most trying student of her 50-year-career. ME!

The rebellious me had reawakened. The duality at home had reactivated, big time! On the outside, we were viewed as a happy, normal, now upper-middle-class family; on the inside, we were self destructing. Dave had just left for college and I had become the only witness to the insanity, but there was no court before which I could testify, no psychiatrists, student counselors, no father confessor. At 13, with my past troubling transgressions, I felt I lacked credibility. I had to grin and bear it alone.

I became a pressure cooker, filled with an explosive, comical brew, which, when mixed with a touch of social hypocrisy, would detonate!

Mrs. Heffernan was teaching U.S. History. She was on a chapter which included our right to petition against grievances. I had "grievances." As I've just said, I couldn't talk about the primary ones at home. So how about grievances at school? That, according to what she was teaching, was fair game. Now until this point I hadn't liked Mrs. Heffernan. She was at least seventy, and often lectured spontaneously on matters other than our lessons. Just at the point when Washington crossing the Delaware was sounding mildly interesting, she'd go off on a tangent about a beautiful river she had seen on her trip to Montana! If it hadn't been that another teacher had instilled a good geography foundation in us, many of my classmates would still believe the American Revolution was largely won in the Rocky Mountains!

There was something else I didn't like about her: she was funny — the worst kind of funny. She was a natural. She could be funny without even knowing it. As Jack Benny would say a few years later on *The Tonight Show, "The secret to comedy is not saying funny things; it's saying things funny."* He was referring to body language and physical and vocal attitude. Mrs. Heffernan was an unconscious master of that. Though advanced in years, her energy and enthusiasm before the class rivaled our own. In the middle of a serious chapter, she would constantly reach under her rather sheer blouse and nervously adjust her "bra strap." It was completely apparent to all of us that she never wore a bra! So as the dead at Gettysburg were being tallied, we, instead of listening, were desperately attempting to stifle our laughter, some of us taking extreme measures to do so. Once I slapped scotch tape over my mouth to prevent a belly laugh from escaping and, of course, this encouraged my fellow student's strong, spontaneous laughter! In show biz we refer to it as a BOFFO!

Mrs. Heffernan's reaction to the sudden interruption was physically funnier than my lead-in! She reacted simultaneously with a look of surprise, then incomprehension, and finally amusement and self delight! It was as if she believed that she had just said or done something hilarious. She was somehow taking credit for my performance! This was act stealing. I would retaliate! The right to petition? So be it!

At lunchtime in the playground, I scribbled at the top of a legal-sized, yellow-lined paper, the words, "This petition is against Mrs. Heffernan!" I had no idea I was supposed to include a detailed description of grievances or the articles of the Constitution which pertained to them.

In twenty minutes I had twenty-nine signatures. Now I may have been *crazy* — but I wasn't *stupid*. I knew that my credibility with our principal, Fred Sherman, was dubious. I had been sent to his office for disciplinary action too many times.

Bill Yacky was our class honor student. I made sure he signed the petition, and insisted he accompany me during its delivery to Mr. Sherman's office. Fred Sherman was no slouch as a principal. I see now that he possessed a wealth of tact, integrity, and wisdom. Some principals may have reacted with *"who do you think you are? You're suspended!"* Mr. Sherman read the petition with genuine concern and consideration, as Yacky and I sat before him at his desk. After a thoughtful moment, he turned to Yacky and asked, "Bill do you really agree with this petition?" To my relief, Bill Yacky also showed signs of developing integrity. "Yes sir, I do. Mrs. Heffernan is often unfair to us, and I'm having trouble following the subject matter, because of the way she teaches." Fred Sherman now had a big problem. In his wisdom, he understood the dynamics of our challenge, which included issues of fairness versus hypocrisy. He knew what history chapter we were studying.

The next afternoon, as we filed into Mrs. Heffernan's class, and took our seats, she was not present. Uncharacteristically, there was a tense silence in the room, interrupted frequently with throat clearing and occasional coughing, reminiscent of the atmosphere at a funeral I had once attended. Nearly all my fellow students had signed my petition and we now sensed a potentially explosive repercussion.

Suddenly, the door flung open and an indignant Mrs. Heffernan thundered in before us. Every spine straightened! All eyes widened! She paced a bit, without saying anything, and then dramatically (she was the best actress I had ever seen), whirled around, an accusing forefinger extended toward all of us, and shouted in deep menacing tones, "I was talking to my neighbor last night! He's a lawyer! And I'm going to *sue* the lot of you!"

At that very moment there was a soft knock on the door. Mr. Sherman stuck his head in: "Mrs. Heffernan?" he asked. "May I please speak to your class alone for a few minutes?" Heffernan then broke into sudden tears, partly it seemed from frustration, but also, I believe, because she realized her threat to sue had been unintentionally overheard by her respected supervisor. She ran, weeping, from the class. This moment was no act. Her genuine humanity was exposed; something we had never seen in her. We gasped and groaned in empathy.

Now it was Mr. Sherman's turn.

"Boys and girls, before I give my decision regarding your petition, I would like to show you something."

He was carrying an 8" x 10" black and white photo, which he asked to be passed from desk to desk as he continued.

"This photograph was taken in 1936. It is a picture of five teachers who were the only ones who came to teach during a very serious active tuberculosis outbreak in our town. All the other teachers stayed home. Out of more than one hundred teachers, these five were the only ones so dedicated to teaching that they risked their lives to come to work. The photograph was taken by our local newspaper, *The Bristol Press*, for an article entitled, "TEACHERS' DEDICATION DESPITE POSSIBLE INFECTION.""

Then he instructed, "Please look at the image of the woman second to the right."

The image referred to was of a young, vibrant Magdelline A. Heffernan, her face displaying a sort of defiant but genuine dignity. My righteous defiance melted into a remorseful goo. Shoulders slumped, I lowered my face to my desk, in an attempt to hide my embarrassment.

"Now, before I share my decision," Sherman continued, "I would like to hear from all of you. What do you think I should do about this situation?"

I was the first to sheepishly raise my hand.

"Gary?"

"I'm at fault. I started this petition, and I hope that everyone will be willing to forget it."

And that was that. There was no retribution. My punishment had been self inflicted. The surprise was that Magdelline A. Heffernan not only began teaching again immediately, but she did so with such clarity and good spirits that she eventually became one of our favorite teachers! In addition, she became my mentor. She called the local newspaper to inform them of the exceptional talent possessed by one of her students. She insisted that a little song which I had written (entitled "He is Good") become the class song at graduation exercises.

He is good
He is fair
He will help us
In despair.

If we're sad
In need of help
We can find it
In a prayer

He is in the raindrops
And the freshly fallen snow
He is in the gardens
That's what makes the flowers grow

He is in this heart of mine
Wherever I may go
He is good
He is God.

I learned a great deal more than American history from Mrs. Heffernan. She demonstrated dignity, forgiveness, and a resiliency of spirit. Those are qualities of a *winner*.

Twenty years later, when I returned to Bristol from Hollywood to do a fund raising performance for the Bristol Boy's Club, my Aunt Adelaide (a school teacher herself) told me to drop by her house after rehearsal. She had someone *special* who wanted to see me. As I walked through the door, there sat Mrs. Heffernan. She was about to celebrate her 93rd birthday. She sat across the room, smiling at me in a way which said: *See, I told them you'd make it.*

I thought she had passed years before. She was still my mentor. God bless her resilient, winning soul.

"TOMORROW"

Tomorrow will be the kind of day
That makes me glad to be alive.
Tomorrow, and when it comes my way
I'll be so happy I survived.

Tomorrow is made of quiet things:
A silent bird with troubles drifting by its wings
The dawn, a satin sunlit stream
A time to dream tomorrow's dream

Tomorrow will be a day so fair
And not the kind that I have known
Tomorrow, there will be someone there
So I'll not ever be alone.

Tomorrow there's a special one
Who'll help me find my way

But tomorrow didn't come again
Today.

— SONG LYRIC BY GARY BURGHOFF
©1965

CHAPTER 5

CR

Our days at Lake Harwington were over. Our Bristol house was for sale. I was a sophomore in Bristol Eastern High School, and I had just been elected president of the class of 1959. I had been taking drumming lessons and had formed my own band. We played at dances around town. Clarence A. Bingham School had done its best for me. Evidently it was good enough. By the time I hit my sophomore year in high school, I was a straight "A" student.

I had struggled through puberty without a whole lot of information about sex from my parents. And, though I didn't know it, I was dangerously ignorant concerning the subject. Many of us in my peer group had formed a sort of mutual masturbation society, and experimentation was, from time to time, happening. Though it seems (by today's standards) relatively innocent, it was, of course, kept secret from our parents.

The girls in 1959 were not "putting out," and the boys knew it. We tested the waters with them, necking in dark corners of movie theaters or back seats of cars. But the mores were largely still Victorian, and the lack of knowledge frightened us. No one dared to tread too deeply into unknown sexual territory. There were too many rumors and innuendos about the consequences of "sinful, sexual behavior." Comedians today tell jokes about the lack of virginity among our young people. In 1959 we were, to my memory, all virgins. If there had been unwanted pregnancies, they must have taken care of it very quietly, because we had no awareness of it except that, now and then, there would be an "early marriage" between 17-, 18-, and 19-year olds. We thought of it as "romantic."

"They tried to tell us we're too young. Too young to really be in love . . ." Nat King Cole summed it up.

I'm not saying we weren't boiling over internally. Our hormones were, at times, making us crazy. But you had to be crazy to do anything about it. Television wouldn't even allow the words "sex" or "pregnant" to be uttered over the airwaves. Sex talk was never appropriate at home (at least not at mine). It was as if our parents were thinking *our lives have enough challenges right now. We'd better not get into the sex thing. Kids have a way of finding out for themselves.*

The schools were playing "Sex-22." Sex was a private matter to be taught at home, but it wasn't, and I think the educators knew it. There were violations. A girlfriend of mine told me that one of our teachers had yanked her into a closet and "felt her up," but she told *me* — not her parents. You just didn't discuss it.

Now, I know that there were probably a lot of things going on in closets around town. Today, gays talk about "coming out"; in 1959 we were all in the closet doing something. In puberty bisexual stimulation was practiced as part of the discovery process. With most it lasted briefly. You grew out of it. We had no idea that the sexual revolution was about to explode. Looking back, it was the passive, irresponsible attitudes of our parent's generation which had lit the fuse.

Anyway, when my testosterone levels reached their peak, I had my drum set in the basement to "beat off on."

One day that spring, I descended the stairs, drumsticks in hand, to find my father, sitting alone on his work stool, and his hands over his face, motionless. I knew instantly his world had collapsed.

"Dad?"

There was a heavy pause.

"I've been fired, Gary. I don't know what to do."

He had worked at the same factory for 30 years. He was a man who defined himself by what he did for a living. He was only forty-six years old, he had never gone to college, and though he was admired among many industrialists and had a good, well-earned reputation, the American post-war clock industry was imploding. Layoffs and cutbacks were going on everywhere. My dad had become a casualty of the times. He knew no other trade, and felt hopeless.

Now, I understood the FOR SALE sign in our front yard. He had seen it coming. And I understood the selling of our beloved summer cottage a few months before. I wasn't yet mature enough to know how to console him. I stood there speechless. He never looked at me; he just got up and went upstairs.

In the weeks to follow, I would learn he had accepted a job offer in Wisconsin, in a little town called Delavan, near the Wisconsin-Illinois border. We were moving.

I was 15. It meant I had to leave the only home I knew. I had finally succeeded in school, was elected president of my class, was just beginning to feel good about myself again, *and* we were moving. I would have been happier living in a tent in a Connecticut campground than moving to Wisconsin. I didn't even know where it was on the map. I would be a *stranger* there. Those Wisconsin kids probably all grew up together. *I had bonded here.* Now I would be the outsider. I felt helpless. My life had been torn apart.

Gripe! Gripe! Gripe! One of the great things about being young is resiliency. I'd be flexible, I'd survive. So we moved.

By the time we had jammed ourselves into Dad's thoroughly over-packed car, and were heading north by northwest, we had sold just about everything we had owned. This included David's '57 Thunderbird sports car he had been given as his high school graduation present. He was attending Pratt Institute of Technology in New York, and majoring in industrial design. He had shown early signs of art talent as a boy in Forestville. I had marveled at his drawings of futuristic boats, airplanes, and automobiles. He also had trouble in school growing up, yet no matter his grade-point average, he always scored an A+ in art. In high school, like me, he had overcome his "inner demons," and excelled. Now, even his reward, for achievement, had to be sold to finance our frantic and apprehensive jaunt into the wilderness.

"THIS TOWN"

I'm gonna git out'a this town
Gonna be big city bound
Gonna finish my schoolin'
And obey their Golden Rule'n
Then I'm 'gonna git out'a this town.

There ain't nothin' to do in this town
'Cep' maybe git blue in this town
Ain't' nothin' to do here
'Cep' hang round getting blue here
I gotta git out'a this town.

Walk to the corner
And hang around there
Whistle at a chick
But that don't git you anywhere
Try to make money
To see where it will git ya'
But ya can't make money
When THE MAN won' let ya'

And this is a bigoted town
The bigots they push you around
Pardon me . . . but that fly is
Free'er than I is.
I gotta git out
I gotta git out
I gotta git out'a this town!

— BLUES LYRIC BY GARY BURGHOFF
©1960

CHAPTER 6

☙

Delavan was a disaster! Not the town. It was a perfectly charming place with friendly and welcoming neighbors. But a week after we arrived, we were hit by a tornado!

My parents had rented a small, temporary house just outside of town. At about 8 a.m., I was awakened by an enormous explosion! Something had violently impacted my bedroom wall! It wasn't my parents fighting. Dad was at work, at his new job, and the impact came from outside. The little house shook so hard, I was knocked out of bed.

"GARY!" My mother screamed from the tiny living room. I rushed to her side before the picture window. We were mesmerized! Out on the street was a car, complete with running motor and driver *in mid air*, just suspended there. It slowly turned, as if by magic, and then came abruptly crashing down upon the road! The driver, who amazingly enough seemed unfazed, simply drove off in the opposite direction from which he had originally been heading. We looked at the sky. It was *GREEN*! Our mouths agape, we just stood there holding onto each other. And then, as suddenly as it came, it ended.

We walked out into the backyard. The "explosion" was caused by a heavy iron patio table, which had been hurled against the house, causing serious damage to my bedroom's exterior wall. I glanced next door. Thirty feet from us our neighbor's patio furniture, made of light folding aluminum, was totally undisturbed.

Welcome to Wisconsin.

I would soon encounter other tornadic activity, but it wouldn't be caused by the weather. It would be caused by culture shock.

I arrived on my first day at Delevan-Darien High School wearing a tweed sports jacket, tie and dress slacks. All of the other students wore long-sleeve plaid shirts and khakis. If my face hadn't looked fifteen, they would have thought I was a teacher! Everyone looked so average. Back in Bristol, our culture had encouraged individualism. Here, normal was the standard.

One of my first classes was physical education. I was jumping around in my shorts and interactively performing exercises (which would make a professional vaudeville contortionist blush) with a group of boys I hadn't even met yet! After I showered, I opened my newly assigned locker and began stocking it with towels, cologne and tennis shoes (called "sneakers" in Connecticut). The locker was small and my shoes wouldn't fit. "What do you do with sneakers here?" I asked the boy standing next to me.

"They get sent to detention," was his answer.

Now in gym, to break the ice, I had relied on my usual formula jokes and one-liners as we exercised. One bizarre maneuver we were forced to perform entailed two of us, one standing on his head and grasping my ankles, while I stood upright grasping his. We then had to begin to roll like a donut, head over heels across the wooden floor. I ended up prostrate; my face firmly pressed against this total stranger's ass! To cover my embarrassment, I began a friendly conversation," Hello, my name is Gary Burghoff, I just blew in from the East Coast. What's your name?" I was speaking directly to his *rectum*. I not only didn't get a laugh, but I was being scrutinized by the gym teacher.

So now, after having gone through my entire repertoire of one-liners during the workout, I'm standing at the locker wondering what "detention" meant when Mr. Zimmerman (the instructor) shouts, "All you Easterners are born with silver spoons in your mouths, aren't you, Burghoff!" I turned to find him in my face, his short stocky frame and pinched beady eyes so close I could smell his skunk-cabbage breath. I thought maybe he was kidding, I didn't know how to react. I hardly knew this guy and all the kids were watching. I hardly knew anybody!

Silver spoons in our mouths? I think I made a stupid and awkward attempt at a comeback line to the effect of, "I guess so . . . among *other places*."

His assault was so violent that it hurled me airborne against and through the solid and very heavy exit door and into the outer hall! I barely landed on my feet and struggled to resist my instinct to return his blow! He passed me smugly along with the other kids and left me standing there bruised and shaking alone in the hall. My whirling brain was frantic to make sense of it. I wasn't being "disruptive." Everyone was chattering, as we bounced each other up and around. It was gym class. They are always noisy. His bitter verbal lashing included "You Easterners," revealing prejudice.

I had been raised to judge others by the content of their character and not their skin tone, religious beliefs or gender and certainly not by their geographic origins! In the area of prejudice, my parents were in total agreement and I respected them for that. What kind of school *was* this? Still shaken, I walked in a daze to my next class. I noticed the plaque on the wall outside a small office with the sign, "Miss Shultz Guidance Counselor."

"Are you Miss Shultz?" I asked, as I entered.

"Ah sure am, you bet. How can I help yah?"

"I'm in trouble and I don't know what to do!"

She was about 30 years of age, her features lacked character and she stood about 5' 5". When I related what Mr. Zimmerman had just done, her response included all sorts of personal questions about my background, dreams, family life and "what job do ya' hope ta git after graduation?" When I told her I aspired to pursue the profession of acting, she started to discourage me! "That doesn't sound like a practical vocation to me. Maybe you should give that one a little more thought, you bet."

This was *guidance*? I came in to report an unprovoked assault by a crazy person and walked out feeling I had just been UNDRESSED. MY confusion and humiliation — not to mention anger — lasted all day.

When I got home after school, my mother was waiting. She had been phoned! "Gary, what did you do? Your Guidance Counselor called."

Still confused, I struggled to relate my perception regarding the facts of the matter.

"That's not what Miss Shultz said. She said you were using perfume and everyone thinks you're a *sissy*!" The perfume was that men's cologne in my locker! I would never have thought to buy it. It was a present from — Guess Who? — *My mom*. I hadn't even opened it. Mom's attention deficit disorder was fully functional and there was no convincing her. And it was suddenly clear that the comedy team of Shultz and Zimmerman had conspired to place blame on me! Needless to say (but I will), trust had become once again one of my dominant issues; not just trust in Mom or the nutcase twins at school, but in the world.

Decades later a good classmate chum of mine, Ron Henriott, who had become Delavan's Mayor, acquiesced, "Do you remember Miss Shultz the Guidance Counselor?"

"Ah, yes."

"She scrambled more students' brains than an eggbeater!"

It took forty years for vindication!

I would now spend the next two and half years of high school regressing and backsliding into my old patterns of rebellion, sagging grades and depression. Not that there wasn't some relief. Some of the teachers were excellent. Willard Strassberger's art class provided a haven for misfits. We would paint away the hour while listening to Mozart and Bach. He was teaching art technique, but the accent was always on beauty and tranquility. One day in class he asked me, "So, what do you intend to enter into the state art competition?" I had no idea what he was talking about. He explained that the Hallmark Greeting Card Company underwrote an annual student art competition in all fifty states. The winner from each state would be honored in Washington with a ceremony and by displaying the fifty winning paintings on the walls of the Library of Congress. The theme chosen was "America Today." I struggled for weeks with ideas, which would visually convey that theme. I did watercolor washes of America cityscapes. I tried painting the people of Delavan in a Norman Rockwell style. Finally, I remembered a line in a book I had read. It was *I Remember Mama*, the classic novel of an American immigrant family, which dealt in part with a mother's love for her daughter, who dreamed of becoming a writer. Through her mother's sacrifice, the girl was finally given an opportunity to be advised by a highly successful author: "Write only what you truly know and love."

Now, like Mrs. Heffernan, I must take you on a tangent.

Back when I had first arrived in town, something wonderful happened. We arrived during prom season and, knowing practically no one, I had no expectation of attending. But, through some contact work by my mother, she had arranged for me to perform a drum solo at the post-prom party, which was to be held in a local nightclub. I had learned to do a flashy Gene Krupa-type routine, which required no musical accompaniment. I guess Mom thought it would be a good way for the kids to get to know me. Well, it was a way of getting attention, anyway. What I didn't know was that there had been a professional big band hired for the affair called The Bud Wilbur Orchestra. While the kids were still at the prom, I arrived and set up my Slingerland drum set (just like the one Gene Krupa played on). Bud Wilbur and the band began to file in. I had set up my drums center stage. There was hardly any room for the musicians. Bud Wilbur approached me to ask, "What are you doing here?"

"I'm doing my drum act to entertain the troops," I explained.

"No offense son, but are you any good?"

I sat at my drums, and wailed away for about five minutes starting low on the high hats and gradually rising to a crescendo, then exploding on the snare drum and tom-toms with a variety of spontainously accented rifts and rolls, which finally ended in a fast machine gun-like display of intensifying triplets all the way to a clamorous cymbal barrage at the finale.

At the sound of the final cymbal crash, I looked up to see a room full of genuine professional side men from some of the most famous swing bands in the country, grinning from ear to ear! They even applauded!

Talk about getting attention! It was a Hollywood fantasy come true!

Wilbur leaned over my tom-tom and said, "Son, you're not going to believe this (I hardly do myself), but our drummer was just in an auto accident on the way over here and is in the hospital. If you're game, after your act, I'd like you to be our drummer for the night." The night was a total success! We jived and swung our way through the night with classic arrangements from Count Basie, Benny Goodman, Duke Ellington, and Gene Krupa. I was in swing paradise! And, though I was rough around all the edges, Bud Wilbur made a fateful decision that night. He asked me to play with them steady. And for all my years in Delavan, I would play professional drums with the "Big Guys" (all sixteen of them) in nightclubs, resorts, proms and dances statewide on weekends and summer vacations. IT WAS A BLAST!

So, back to my art project and *writing what you know and love* . . . It occurred to me that, if that worked for *writing*, it should also be true for painting. *Let's see*, I thought, *What do I know and love that is typically and originally American?*

Duh! My painting was called "Men of Jazz." It was a watercolor-and-pen rendition of a jazz quartet playing cool jazz in a smoke-filled nightclub. I had developed a unique "scribble" technique of my own to accomplish it. With India ink and a fountain pen, I very spontaneously scribbled all over the canvas in aggressive sweeping strokes without ever allowing the pen point to lose contact with the surface until I began to see the subject matter emerging. In other words, I was in a sense allowing the composition to create itself. Once I could see the musicians emerging from the scribbling, I then only needed to enhance them with color, modeling and detail.

A few weeks had passed since I submitted my painting to the state judges when Willard Strassberger casually dropped an official-looking letter on my desk. I assumed it contained a "thank you *but*" message. But when I opened it, to my amazement, the first and most important word was "CONGRATULATIONS." I had won!

Without even trying, I had achieved something important! I would have to be careful not to let that happen too often. I wouldn't want to damage my developing image as a rebellious loser. It didn't occur to me then that the commitment and weeks of work that I had devoted produced an achievement as valuable as getting an "A" in algebra. Art was something you enjoy doing. I was sure that didn't count on my parent's "achievement list." I remember thinking, *I guess I'm safe enough . . . for now.*

There were other havens. Bob Spevicek's music class was teaching me discipline. All the other percussionists in "band" (as it was called) were excellent readers. Though I was playing professionally on weekends, I couldn't even keep up with following the measures on the written page. I'd constantly nudge the drummer next to me, asking where we were. But Spevicek was patient and, before long, my reading skills improved. They would be needed. In two years I would become a songwriter in New York while I struggled to study acting and awaiting my "big break."

By 1960 I was not only swinging on the weekends, I was in full swing in school. My dress clothes were now reserved only for church on Sunday and even Mr. Zimmerman's gym class had become tolerable. My grades, except for art and band, had not improved. If I scored a D+, I considered myself triumphant. My parents had just about given up hope and that meant (I thought) less pressure and griping at home. My unconscious resolve to deny either of them the benefit of my achievements had become a total success! And though that negative resolution often led me into long and gloomy bouts with depression and insecurity, I had become accustomed to it and regarded it as normal.

There was only one black person in our school. His name was Mike Kennedy. He reminded me of a good friend I had known when I was a boy in Forestville. My little playmate's name was Walter Pitkie, whose name I used in the song "I Made It." But the song didn't do Walter justice. He was the kind of kid you just had to like; easygoing, kind, and fun to be around. If you cracked a joke at someone else's expense (something of which I was often guilty), Walter would not think it funny. His heart was too good. And though I was "all screwed up," I had respect for him. Mike Kennedy was like that. He was bright, polite, had a gentle sense of humor, and was a pleasure to be around.

One afternoon in Mr. Havler's social studies class, the subject turned to Civil Rights. Mike was seated at the desk in front of me. I raised my hand to ask, "If a Negro man and a white man both scored the same on their application to teach here, which would be hired?"

Without hesitation, Havler responded, "The white man."

Now I had him. I continued with a follow-up: "What if the black man scored much higher?"

I fully expected him to thoroughly consider the second part of my question. Instead, he immediately and cavalierly responded with "The white man."

Mike and I looked at each other in total shock. "WHY?" I asked with increased intensity. His final response was, without him knowing it I'm sure, so hurtful and alarming to our young minds, it profoundly changed the way we viewed the world. His casual but devastating reply of, *"Because that's the way it is"* made my

16-year-old blood boil! I could only imagine how Mike felt. Though he was bright and vibrant, I, for the first time, sensed how he was forced into passivity. It had been demanded of him in this or any American town all his life. I wanted him, with the defiant dignity he possessed, to . . . *do what?* Get up and walk out? That also was passive. Leap from his seat and strangle Mr. Havler? So much for dignity. How about reciting the Gettysburg Address? *No!* He had to, for the moment, for all his life's moments, swallow his pride and take it! And that's what good and wholesome Negroes had been doing for 300 years. I knew there was injustice. I had visited my grandparents, my mother's mom and step-grandfather in the South. We had viewed with disgust the signs on the drinking fountains marked, "COLORED ONLY," the tarpaper shanties, and most of all, the utter rudeness of the attitudes.

Jim Crow was alive and unfortunately very well in the South and in some ways even worse in the North. The South declared it at every public soda fountain, every school, movie theater or public park. In the North it was hidden and surfaced in "jokes" and snide comments between whites at exclusive country clubs and tea parties. My family had seen the injustice but we also were at fault. Though we were appalled by the coy, hateful comments, we didn't speak out and, to the bigot, our silence signaled tacit approval.

In 1960, decent white Americans were due for an awakening. We only needed a spark to ignite the Revolution. At the moment, Mr. Havler uttered, "Because that's the way it is," I wanted to be that spark.

The next Saturday morning I found myself walking the tidy, ordered neighborhood streets just off Delavan's main drag. A friend, Lonnie Little, approached me. "Hey, there's some guy giving a speech on the back of a hay wagon over in front of the hotel." As I walked the two blocks to the hotel, I could see the small crowd which had gathered. They were all local adults and were listening to a tall, good-looking man, who was standing on the back of a farm truck. As I assimilated among the fifteen or so that had gathered, they were discussing farm issues and concerns about the economy. I had no idea who this guy was or what office he might be running for; dog catcher, for all I knew. But I had a piece to speak, and though I feared the reaction from the adults around me, those who

I had to live among for the next two years, I was determined to speak it.

Suddenly, my will faltered. It is hard to imagine today with racial rhetoric commonplace and often so prevalent that it is taken for granted, but I had never spoken out before. Would I appear foolish? I was stricken with fear and insecurity. I had to screw up my courage to finally raise my nervous, trembling hand. Though my impetus was strong, I was disappointed at the weakness of my wavering voice as I spoke.

After the speaker acknowledged me, I said, "If you are elected, what do you intend to do about the unfairness and injustice suffered by Negroes?"

For what seemed an eternity to me, the crowd was hushed. The handsome speaker, with eyes that seemed to penetrate deep within you, just paused and looked at me. A woman next to me, sensing my nervousness and wanting to ease the moment, said "Yeah, how about that?" My face must have turned tomato red and so did the speaker's who I sensed was empathizing with my embarrassment. His stare turned into a warm look of delight and his smile foretold his response.

"If I'm elected President, I promise that one of my first actions will be the writing and introducing of a Civil Rights Bill which will, once and for all, guarantee that all people will have equal opportunity under the Declaration of Independence and the Constitution of the United States."

It was John Kennedy.

To my surprise, my Delavan neighbors broke into spontaneous applause.

In retrospect, if I had not spoken out, this great man might not have, in that place, thought the subject appropriate, and my neighbors' response would not have revealed to him the entrapped sentiments of these decent average white Americans, who like me, harbored feelings that had remained too silent, too long.

I have often wondered if, after his election, when he sat, pen in hand, to endeavor to keep his promise, he remembered that nervous, insecure 16-year-old, who had to overcome a lifetime of unconscious oppression to speak. In some small way, did it add to the courage which he possessed in abundance? Did I make a difference, speaking out?

Mike Kennedy, my friend, had deserved as much. John Kennedy, our President, would represent our hope.

"IT'S A GREAT WORLD"

It's a great world, after all
It hasn't changed that much
You can still find the wonder, if you want to
And she's got a wonderful touch!

It's a great life after all
You simply have a choice
You can still hear lovely music, if you listen
And she's got the loveliest voice!
Everything's coming up clear now
Ever since she came my way
Here comes that "Happy New Year" now
That I laughed at yesterday!

It's a great world when you care
And live to give your all
To somebody special who is waiting
With a love that's ten feet tall!

Cause when someone special is waiting
IT'S A GREAT WORLD AFTER ALL!

— SONG LYRIC BY GARY BURGHOFF
©1965

CHAPTER 7

CR

I had graduated! My senior year had passed at the exasperating speed of a stream of coagulating glue. At graduation exercises, I had accepted my diploma gleefully, believing my "C minus" grade point average a victory. Though my father had repeated the words, "These are the best years of your life" so many times; I was ready to scream, the relief of knowing it was over was liberating! Now I had *my* life ahead of me. *These* years would be my best.

It was 1962. JFK had been elected against Richard Nixon (whom my parents supported), and a new spirit, as refreshing as honeysuckle in a pigpen, was sweeping the country. "Ask not what your country can do for you; ask what you can do for your country . . ." invited us to participate in healing the wounds inflicted on minorities. The Peace Corps was inspiring voluntary hands-on participation abroad improving the infrastructure of "third world nations." Good will and acts of international kindness and understanding were beginning to show results so positive that in spite of the nightmarish psychological effects of nuclear proliferation between America and the Soviet Union, we had begun to hope! We were even going to the moon! And I was going to Hollywood—via New York.

I had been performing in plays and musicals at the Belfry Theater in Williams Bay (a stone's throw from Delavan) during the summers. The well-known little church, which had been converted to a summer stock theatre, had sparked the early career of Paul Newman. My mother and other guest directors were hired to guide us through plays and musicals such as Rodgers and Hart's *Babes in Arms*, Sandy Wilson's *The Boy Friend*, and Peter Ustinov's *Romanoff and Juliet*.

My performance as the outrageous, temperamental southern director in *Babes in Arms* won me the Belfry "Bell" award as Best Supporting Actor in a comedy musical; all of this reinforcing my resolve to make acting my life.

A young actor who appeared in several productions Mom had choreographed fell in love with another member of the cast in the summer of 1961. I have mentioned Mom's generosity. The young actor was so broke Mom financed his honeymoon. It was years later that I learned that that this impoverished actor was Harrison Ford!

Though Paul Newman's contribution to the Belfry legend had been accomplished many years earlier, the story was still being passed around. He had joined his castmates for dinner at a local restaurant after a tiring rehearsal. The yet-unknown actor had been ejected because he was not wearing a tie (a pretentious practice of many restaurants at the time). Newman, who was becoming known for his righteous rebelliousness, went back to the costume room at the Belfry and after selecting an appropriate necktie, returned to the restaurant's entrance. But the tie was all he was wearing! He was otherwise totally naked. I had hoped the story was true. He sounded like my kind of guy.

One of the hired directors in the summer of 1961 had been a man named Frank Davidson. He was head of the Drama Department at New York's City College. My mom worked with him as choreographer for musical productions and, as always, was "networking" for me. By midsummer, Davidson had seen my work and agreed to recommend me to the famous acting teacher, Sanford Meisner, and the newly formed Musical and Dramatic Theater Academy in New York where Sanford was head of the acting department. I had just turned 19.

Today, having children of my own, and having gone through the worrisome process of easing them into a life of "independence," I reflect with total sympathy on my parents' challenge. With one of their boys already in his fourth year at Pratt (and me waiting in the wings), that challenge must have been formidable.

Dad's position as Vice-President of the Borg Company in Delavan yielded less salary than he had known in Bristol. By the time my turn to leave the nest had come, there was little left for my education. I had a year, maybe two, to make my mark.

Frank Davidson (bless him) agreed to house me in his apartment on mid-Manhattan's fashionable Park Avenue for a week or so until I could find a room of my own. On a Monday morning in the autumn of 1962, my bags were packed and my exhausted parents, much more anxious than I, inserted me into a taxi cab with $300 in my pocket along with two suitcases and other meager belongings and handed "Red," Delavan's lone cab driver, the address of the Chicago train station. After tearful "goodbyes" and hugs, and as the cab began to back out of our driveway, my dad spontaneously shared the wisest advice he could muster: "Don't be a chorus boy." He probably kicked himself as soon as I was gone. I felt like kicking him myself! *What the hell did he mean?* I would spend the next two days on a train to New York speeding toward the answer to my life's dream and instead of reveling in my sudden independence and my hopes of a bright and exciting future, I spent the whole trip doubting my own sexuality!

When I finally reached my destination of New York's Grand Central Station, I phoned Frank's office to make him aware of my arrival. His secretary read a note he had left for me:

"Meet me at my apartment at 6:30 this evening."

It was 11:00 a.m.; I had seven hours to see New York. I grabbed a cab and asked to be let off anywhere as long as it was Broadway!

As I walked New York's most famous street, I was astounded at the immensity of it all. There must have been a half a million people on Broadway that day. New York can change your perspective and do so very quickly. While I was a "star" at the Belfry, I was a flea in an elephant's ear here. I felt lost and frightened among the passing throng.

Suddenly, among all these thousands of New Yorkers, I saw a familiar face! It was Red, the Delavan, Wisconsin cab driver who had taken me to the Chicago train station two days earlier.

"Red!" I yelled, "What the hell are you doing here?"

"As I was driving you to the station, you made your trip to New York sound so exciting that, after I dropped you off in Chicago, I just kept driving East 'til I got here to see for myself!" he replied. "My wife doesn't even know I'm gone yet!"

I remember remarking, "Why didn't you take me with you?"

Within a half-hour I had made my way over to the Radio City Music Hall. There standing in line to get in was Don Fornier, my drum teacher from Bristol! Suddenly New York City and the world seemed very small again.

In the days which followed, Frank Davidson helped me through a hundred apartment-for-rent ads in the *New York Daily News* classifieds. Finally, I rented a room in an apartment for $85 per month on the fifth floor of an old brownstone building at 68th Street and Second Avenue on New York's East Side. Having already registered at the academy, I was to begin my acting classes the following morning.

I shared the apartment with Mr. Oliva and his ninety-year-old mother, Maria. Mr. Oliva was from South America and a Spanish interpreter at the United Nations. His favorite comedian was "Red *Skeleton*." I remember hoping that he wasn't interpreting any matters which might concern a nuclear arms attack.

As my alarm sounded at 7:00 a.m. the next morning, I leapt from bed, dressed and ran for a subway station. This was it! My time to make my mark had arrived! I was heading for my first day at acting school and stardom. I was determined to be the first one there on East 23rd Street when their doors opened at 9 a.m.

I ran down the nearest subway stairs, paid my fifteen cents and took a seat as the train sped off. Now, I had never taken a subway before and I was on the wrong train! In forty-five minutes, I realized my mistake and frantically sought a conductor for information. There are no conductors on subway trains!

The numbers of the stops had increased from 68th Street to 123rd Street! When the doors opened, I ran from the train up the stairs and onto the street. I was in Harlem! I checked my watch. It was 8:35. Frantically, I asked the first person I saw directions to East 23rd Street.

"Hey, man. You all screwed up. Take dat subway ova dair. You need to go sout!"

I was out of breath when I took a seat on the southbound train, and hadn't noticed the "Bronx" sign on the front. About the time we were passing under the East River, I was contemplating suicide.

I arrived at school at 2:15 p.m. I had rushed to get there at a cost of $1.50 in fifteen-cent fares! It took me five hours. My new sharkskin suit jacket was wet in the armpits with perspiration as I entered Phillip Burton's office. Phillip was actor Richard Burton's surrogate father and director of the Academy. When I apologized and explained what happened, he responded with "Pardon my asking Mr. Burghoff, but did you come to New York to study the theatre or the entire New York subway system? Perhaps you should, instead of acting, be studying civil engineering!"

On my first day, I had made an impression . . . and it wasn't good. By the time I left his office, my last class was already in progress and rather than interrupting it with my late arrival, I took the next subway train home to 68th Street.

By now, I knew how the subway worked and I had no trouble finding my way back. But trouble had found *me* and wasn't finished with me yet. I climbed the long five flights of stairs and reached into my pocket for the keys to the apartment. I had placed them in my jacket's inside pocket; the jacket which I had removed and placed on the seat next to me on the homebound train; the jacket which had fallen off the seat of the homebound train. My apartment keys were on their way to Harlem again! As I was knocking on the apartment door, I noticed a small note Mr. Oliva had taped there. "Well Gary Burgoof, you have the place to yourself! We have gone to visit friends. Be back next week." I had sudden visions of sleeping in the hall for a week!

The only other person I knew was an elderly Italian woman who sold flowers at the florist across 68th Street. I ran down the stairs and across the street to her shop. When I explained my conundrum, she said, "Oh yeah, you — gotta — da-big — a-problem!" She removed a large screwdriver from behind the counter. "You takah-dah-driva-an-climah-upah-da-roof! You-climah-downah-da-fire-scapah-inah-dah-alley. Wen-you-getah-toyou-window, you-pry-ah-open!" It sounded a little dangerous, but entirely reasonable. My dad had locked us out of our house in Wisconsin and had pried open a window with a similar screwdriver. The hard part, I thought, was climbing all those stairs again.

The heavy metal door, which led onto the roof, was unlocked. As I walked upon the soft, warm, gummy tar, my eyes searched for the fire-escape stairs. Finding them, I made my descent. There were seven stories to my building. So I had only to descend two of them to reach our kitchen window which faced the narrow alley between ours and the neighboring brownstones. But as I passed the seventh-story window, there in full view, stood a half-dressed, middle-aged woman cooking a steak on a hot plate. Our eyes met. If I had been wearing a hat, I would have tipped it to reassure her I meant no harm. No hat, just an embarrassed grin and a sudden diverting of my eyes.

By the time I reached the sixth story, I was hearing windows opening across the narrow alley behind me. But when I turned to see the origin of the sound, they all slammed shut simultaneously.

Subconsciously, I heard the faint sound of a siren on the street out front. Finally, I reached the fifth-story window. I recognized the bouquet of flowers on the kitchen table I had bought my landlady on the previous day. I was home! Now for prying open the decaying, paint-chipped window. After a few tries and much noise, the old swivel latch popped apart and the window slid open. I had done it! Well, almost. The kitchen door was closed and locked from the hall outside. I peered through the antiquated keyhole and saw that the key had been left inserted in the other side. There was a *New York Times* on the counter. I had seen it a thousand times in "B" movies! I slid the paper under the door and with the screwdriver, pushed out the key onto the newspaper and pulled it back toward me in the kitchen. It was a snap. I unlocked the kitchen door and proceeded immediately down the hall and out the front door leaving it ajar behind me.

On my way down the stairs (I was going down to return the screwdriver) there, blocking my path on their way up, were two of the biggest policeman I had ever seen! And their guns were drawn! I froze, they froze; their guns held with both hands down toward the stairs.

"Were you just up on that roof?" one of them aggressively shouted.

"Yes, but . . ."

They raised their guns!

"Drop your weapon!"

My . . . my . . . *weapon?*" My God! They mean the stupid screwdriver!

I dropped it immediately. It bounced once on the landing and ricocheted toward them down the stairs. Holstering their guns, they leapt at me, one grabbing me in a headlock, the other holding my feet. As they carried me down the remaining four flights of stairs, I remember shouting, "Hey take it easy, I live here!" But my cries were drowned by other voices below in the echoing stairwell.

"Did ya get 'em . . . get 'em?" came a voice from an unknown location.

"Yeah, we got 'em . . . ot 'em," answered the one who held my feet.

"Was he armed? . . . armed?"

"Yeah . . . a screwdriver! . . . iver!"

By this time we were in the entrance lobby, I counted five more police officers. I could see the flashing lights on their cruiser through the windows of the entrance door. As they carried me out to the awaiting police vehicle, I shouted, "Please, I live here. It's my apartment!"

They paused for a moment and a more distinguished senior member asked, "What's your apartment number?"

I was so terrified of being arrested, I had forgotten it! "Wait a minute . . . I know it . . . just give me a second to remember . . ."

They didn't wait! The cruiser door flung open, and I was being hurled headfirst into the back seat, as I shouted, "5-B!"

"Hold it!" shouted the distinguished one. "Give him a chance to talk."

I was at the point of tears: "Look, I just moved in yesterday. If you bring me back upstairs to the apartment, I'll prove I live here!"

Believe it or not, proving you live in a room in someone else's apartment wasn't as easy as it sounded. The first thing they saw was the apartment door left ajar, something you just don't do in New York, not if you live there. Next, after entering, two of them held me against the entry hall wall, as the others searched every corner of the apartment. I wasn't allowed to escort them into my room. Now came the interrogation.

"If you live here, describe the food in the refrigerator!"

I had no idea; the food belonged to the Olivias! I stood there speechless. *Oh, God*, I thought to myself, *they're going to put me in jail!*

"Should we run him in now?" asked my captor to my left.

"No, wait a minute," said the senior officer. "Son, I want to be fair. What can you identify in this apartment?"

Upon moving in the day before, I had bought and installed an aquarium in my room.

"Guppies," I said.

"*GUPPIES?*" responded the gray-haired father figure.

"Four Guppies. Three males. One female. One of the males has a fantail . . . yellow, purple and orange. The others have colored, spotted bodies and the female is larger and dull gray. Also, a Placostumous. He's strange looking and attaches his suction-cup-like mouth to the inside of the glass. They're algae eaters. In addition, there are four Neon Tetras, a Red Molly, and two Leopard Catfish!"

Are you burglars reading this? The moment you break into a house, before you steal anything, be sure to check to see if it contains an aquarium. Then take the time to memorize its contents. If the police catch you, you'll be released immediately! Fortunately, among the seven members of New York's finest, was a young officer who was also an amateur ichthyologist! As I was rattling off my list of aquatic occupants, he had entered my room.

"He's right . . . in every detail."

One of his tougher-looking cohorts said, "How the hell would you know?"

A little embarrassed, the junior officer said defensively, "I like fish . . . I have an aquarium at home!" After the first silent moment in fifteen minutes, he continued: "*What?* — a cop can't like fish? . . . *They relax me!*"

By now I could clearly see the word "Lieutenant" struck on the gold and silver badge of the older one. He began to giggle, his eyes beginning to water, his face turning suddenly red. In a second, he was reeling with laughter.

"Okay, son," he said, "we believe you, but the next time you lock yourself out, you call *us* . . . you understand!"

"Yes, sir. You bet I will."

They were laughing and shaking their heads in disbelief as they exited the apartment. I suddenly felt as if I was saying goodnight to a group of poker buddies I had just told a funny joke to.

But the toughest one wasn't laughing. He, being the last one out the door, turned before he left and said, "You know, when the call came in, I was outside on your corner. I watched you climb down that fire escape with my .357 Magnum pointed right up your kazoo. I could have killed you." He turned and left without another word.

I bolted the Olivas' three-door locks behind them and, with hand over my pounding heart and knees buckling, I staggered to my room and fell face down on my bed. The phone rang. It was my ever-intuitive mom back in Wisconsin.

"Hello, Gary. I just called to make sure you moved into a safe neighborhood. I hope your apartment is near a police station."

"Don't worry, Mom . . . it is."

So ended my first day at acting school.

∽   ∽   ∝   ∾   ∾

On my second first day of acting school, Sanford Meisner asked our class, "How many of you have performed in high school plays and local theater?"

Nearly the whole class raised their hands.

"JESUS CHRIST! AM I GOING TO HAVE TROUBLE WITH *THIS* CLASS!" he groaned.

He had begun on a positive note, don't you think?

Fortunately, during most of the week, the real acting class was taught by a wonderful, compassionate man named James Tuttle. Sanford had formed a select team of acting teachers from his well of ex-students, who were skilled in teaching his very brilliant and unique method of study. Jim would conduct the class all week. Then every Monday we would show our progress to Sanford in his private classroom.

When the famous Russian author and theatre master, Stanislovski, published his immortal novel, *An Actor Prepares*, decades earlier, he had ignited a revolution in the acting art. His powers of observation as to what made great actors real on stage rivaled the genius of Freud and Einstein. Suddenly, actors were learning to live their characters' lives instead of just playing them. The accent had changed from dramatic declaratory acting to a new realism. This may sound like a simple task, but anyone who thinks acting is easy, doesn't know the first thing about it.

The highly disciplined acting games, which Sanford had devised, were exercises designed to teach us the principles of concentration, emotional and physical spontaneity, sense memory (an advanced exercise in emotional recall which merges your inner self with the character you are playing), and finally, how to apply all this training to the artificial environment of a stage or before the lens of a movie camera.

We worked in Jim's class for five months on the first and most basic exercise called "the word game" before we were considered ready to add the second exercise. When, after extensive study, you had mastered all the exercises you had learned the basics of improvised, moment-to-moment *organic acting* and you were ready to apply it to "scene-study," performing actual scenes from existing plays before the class. The total process took years!

Sanford had forbidden us to even audition for professional roles for the first two years. He knew that, regardless of our talent, we wouldn't be ready.

Now, while a brilliant teacher, Meisner in my experience at least, was a dreadful human being. He possessed a rude and destructive personality which destroyed the confidence of the young students he had taken in.

In my case, I was placed on his "shit list" very early on.

Some of the students who were aspiring playwrights, had composed a satirical "roast"-like review, which exaggerated outrageously our teachers' foibles and imperfections. They came to me to ask if I would play Sanford. The review was scheduled to be performed at the school's annual Christmas Party.

For very good emotional reasons, I have long ago blocked out of my memory the actual scene I played portraying Meisner before the entire faculty. But it was anything but flattering. Afterward, Meisner refused to allow me to work in his class, ever again. As each acting team would, in their turn, be chosen to perform a scene before him, he would always pass me by. Finally, after two months, he turned to me and sarcastically asked, "Are you still doing impersonations of me at parties?"

Trying to choke my emotions, I responded, " Mr. Meisner, I didn't write the material; I just played it to the best of my ability."

"I know," he said. "That's why, instead of expelling you, I'm going to continue ignoring you!"

Jim Tuttle, who always sat next to Sanford at his desk, slammed down his notebook so explosively it sent Sanford fearfully flying off his chair! Tuttle stormed out of the classroom leaving all his student notes behind — and he would never come back! That evening after school, I phoned him to ask if he was all right.

"Gary," he said "though it may have seemed spontaneous, my outburst and resignation was well planned in advance! I did just as I wanted. That brilliant but cruel S. O. B. has discouraged too many talented young people for too long. I've already rented a loft in midtown Manhattan and I'm going out on my own. I'll faithfully teach his method by myself, but I'll be damned if I'll be a continued witness to his cruelty."

By the following afternoon, about fifteen percent of my class had handed in their "resignations" and enrolled in Jim's new acting program . . . he would teach Sanford's method, better than Sanford. I was the first to make the switch.

"HERE'S MY SONG"

Here's my song — It's a new one
A sad one, but a true one
A blue one, cause' you broke my heart today

It's a simple refrain from a broken heart
To let you know I've flown away.

Like a bird, flying out there
Passed the clouds, high about there
Passed the sun, to the highest shooting star

Where this bluebird, is a new bird
Shining from afar

Here's my song of goodbye then
May the teardrops from my eyes then
Turn to raindrops that will wash your fear away
May that shooting star above you
Always light your way.

— SONG LYRIC BY GARY BURGHOFF
©1963

CHAPTER 8

CR

On the morning of November 22, 1963, I was awakened by a phone call from a student friend, Ray Gorley.

"Gary . . . Have your heard?"

"Heard what?"

"The President, he's been shot!"

"How . . . how can that be?"

"Turn on the television. They think he's dying!"

The shock and disbelief led instantly to denial. I refused to believe John Kennedy would die! He was more than our vague hope for peace and fairness. He personified our youth and idealism and the belief that anything our hearts could project toward a better world could be accomplished. He was the brother you emulated, the father you were proud of, and the shining star which led the way to our future.

It is hard today to convey to my children all that he meant to us who had felt liberated and finally free; not just because of his integrity and his politically forward-looking policies, but because unlike the other presidents we had known, we loved him — as a man. I loved him. He was my hero.

There was a soft knock on my door.

"Mister Gary, oh . . . Mr. Gary. . ."

I opened it to find ninety-year-old Mrs. Oliva standing there; her arms outstretched to me, her face wet with tears. I knew he had died and with him, my young and hopeful heart. I fell into her arms. Though she spoke no English, her consoling and tender embrace conveyed the sweeter essence of humanity.

Hope would no longer lighten our path. A new cynicism would take its place. God and the angels would weep. Bobby, Malcolm and Martin would follow, and with them, our collective broken hearts and innocence.

"BE PRACTICAL"

Be practical and fall in love
Be practical go out and lose your heart
Be practical and spend your lifetime on a dream- a scheme

Responsible for all you love
Responsible, no matter how they laugh — gotta be
Responsible, respond by living for your dream.

Words are funny things
You sometimes can be fooled
People twist them so that
Love is overruled!

So be practical and save your dreams
Be practical and lock them in your heart
Be practical but never throw away the key!

Someone a world apart
May love your dreamer's heart
Someone "practically" like me.

— SONG LYRIC BY GARY BURGHOFF
©1963

CHAPTER 9

℞

My parents were worried. By the time my 3rd year of acting classes rolled around, the money they had saved for my schooling and living expenses was long since spent.

Dad was increasingly calling me and begging me to choose a more PRACTICAL direction for my life.

"You'd make a hell of a sales-rep for the factory."

"But, Dad, I'm an actor."

"Oh, you just want to do . . . what you WANT to do!" was his strange and frustrated reply.

Was I expected to do something I DIDN'T want to do as my life's work? What kind of reasoning was that?

I now realize that, to my father's generation who had suffered the Great Depression of the 20's and 30's, a job — any job — defined you as a man. But my acting skills were becoming well developed and all I needed was my "Big Break" to show the world what I could contribute.

In the meantime, I sold underwear at Saks on Fifth Avenue and worked as an usher in a movie house.

One day I remembered that I was still an active member of A. F. of M. (The American Federation of Musicians Union). I went to Union Hall and placed my résumé (listing my Big Band experience from my Bud Wilbur gigs) on the bulletin board. To my surprise, my phone began ringing immediately and I was soon playing with jazz and dance combos in little bars and clubs throughout Manhattan. In those days, if you made $300 a week you could get by, and that became easy for me. Best of all, playing in nightclubs left my days free for auditioning.

There was a new musical being planned. It was originally called "Dolly, A Most Exasperating Woman." But, during the auditioning process, David Merrick, its producer, changed the title to "Hello Dolly!" I was not yet a union actor. Fortunately, the stage union (Actors Equity Association) insisted on "open calls" for non-union actors once the union pros had auditioned. In this way, new talent could have a chance to emerge increasing the union's number of working stage actors.

My first audition was for Merrick himself! I worked for weeks preparing a song with my show-tune accompanist, Pat Nugent. I would sing, "There's A Lot of Living to Do" from one of Merrick's pervious hit musicals, *How to Succeed in Business (Without Really Trying)*.

One evening I asked James Tuttle if he would drop over to Nugent's studio to advise me during a rehearsal. Jim heard my performance, but was unimpressed.

"Gary, lie down on the floor and do your relaxation exercise." (Tension is the actor's enemy on stage; it prohibits spontaneity and emotional expression.)

I lay down flat on my back and allowed all my muscles to relax as if they were becoming one with the floor.

"Now, plug in all the important yearnings and expectations you feel. Be personally specific as to the things which represent success to you: *A flashy car? See it specifically. . . a warm, lovely woman to share your life . . . See a specific face . . .having money . . . Specifically see your bank as you walk in to make a withdrawal . . .* Now . . . speak the words to the song."

As I lay there, my eyes closed; I began . . .

> "There are girls — just ripe for some kissin'
> And I mean to kiss me a few
> Oh, those girls don't know what they're missin'
> There's such a lot of living to do! . . ."

"Now, sing the rest," said Jim softly while signaling Pat to play.

> "And there's WINE all ready for tasting!
> And there's CADILLACS, all shining and new
> GOT TO MOVE, cause time is a wastin'
> I got a lot of living to do!"

While before I had just been singing my chosen audition piece, I was now LIVING IT! It made all the difference in the delivery. Now, when I performed it the following afternoon before David Merrick, he would be seeing and feeling my own unique qualities. My true youthful yearnings, ambition and restlessness streaming through the song he had heard sung a thousand times.

Producers don't want singers — they want *actors* who can sing. It worked. The impression I made at the audition narrowed me down to only five of a hundred hopefuls. But, in the end Jerry Dodd, another actor with more Broadway experience, got the job. *Hello Dolly!* would become the most successful musical in history . . . *without Gary Burghoff*! Though Merrick's office would ask me to audition for all the Dolly Companies, which went out worldwide, I would never be hired.

Other auditions were happening on nearly a daily basis. I auditioned for strange experimental off-Broadway plays, horribly written musicals, summer stock jobs in faraway places, for directors who cast in New York.

My first professional summer stock job paid me $19 per week and I had to kick back $10 a week for my room. The little theater in New Hampshire was doing "ten in ten." That meant utilizing the same cast members who performed ten musicals in ten weeks! And, *that* meant we were rehearsing all day for the next production while performing a full musical production every night. You had about five hours to sleep each night. *Easy?* You better believe it was *not*! It was a super-human effort, which we, without complaint, sailed through. Such is the dedication of young actors.

At many auditions, I would bump into a rising star and uniquely talented woman named Barbara Minkus. We were called frequently because casting directors had identified us as talented, but "offbeat" types. So we were called to audition for the more bizarre, offbeat shows.

I was not only playing drums for a living, I also had been hitting the streets on Tin Pan Alley as an aspiring songwriter. One publisher, Hal Webbman at the Larry Spear Company, heard the demo recording of my song, "Tomorrow," and hired me on the spot. Hired? He offered to throw me $50 bucks a week to hang around the office teaming up with other hopeful writers who sometimes, but rarely, came up with a hit record.

Before long, I was receiving royalties for two songs I had written which Hal had recorded. I'd mention their titles, but you wouldn't recognize them — Oh, what the hell, "My Heart, Your Heart" and "Roses and Rainbows." My total royalties for both releases amounted to eighty-nine cents.

But, I had joined ASCAP (American's Society of Composers, Authors and Publishers), which is a protective organization and not a union. My first dues payment, upon entry, was $10. Four days later, I received a check from ASCAP for $60 in profit sharing. My salaries from my band work, songwriting and ASCAP checks grossed me about $400 a week. I was doing all right for an otherwise starving New York actor in 1967.

Nonetheless, late that year I sat, on a rainy spring day, looking out the window of my tiny studio apartment, onto a drab, wet 89th Street, where I had moved a year earlier.

My parents, my brother and all my family back home had given up hope that I would ever succeed. What's worse, so had I.

I called Mom and Dad and asked if I could "visit" them in Wisconsin for a week. (I'd stay months.)

What had seemed the last straw was losing my final bid for the Jerry Dodd part in the Mary Martin London Company of *Hello Dolly!* I had also been studying with Charles Nelson Reilly who had a unique and excellent musical comedy class at H. B. Studios. Jim Tuttle, in my fifth year, feeling he had taught me all he could, had sent me to Charles as a "Finishing" Course. It was no fault of Charles' that I was feeling FINISHED. He was the kindest man and teacher a young student could have ever hoped for. His class tied together nicely the serious theater techniques I had learned with the musical-comedy experience. And Charles was one of the stars in the original cast of *Hello Dolly!* with Carol Channing on Broadway.

When he heard I'd been called back to audition (this time for the famous Director/Choreographer, Gower Champion . . . *himself*), Charles insisted on coaching me. He felt that Gower was probably looking for a carbon copy of Jerry Dodd's characterization of "Barnaby" (the 4th banana role I had long sought). So for a week Charles taught me the exact dance routines Gower had choreographed for Jerry.

When I finally auditioned for Gower, he said, "I think we have a misunderstanding. I'm looking for a new, original approach, Gary. You're just copying Jerry!"

Though he gave me another day to work out my own dance routine, once again, the role went to another who had more Broadway experience. What made it more crushing at this negative time in my "career" was a call from Charles from the payphone at Sardi's, (New York's celebrity restaurant), about three weeks later.

"Gary — it's Charles. I just thought it might cheer you up to know that Gower just stopped by my table to say — and this is confidential — after rehearsing the other actor they hired, he thinks they should have hired *you!*"

While Charles was being his usual supportive and optimistic self, I was so depressed at this point, I viewed what he had just said as proof; God Himself did not want me to succeed! Continuing to pay my apartment rent ($125 a month), I took the next plane back to Wisconsin.

It would take me six months before I'd learn the greatest lesson of my life.

God doesn't give you what you want, when you want it. He gives you what you NEED, when you NEED IT! He was about to drop my "Big Break" directly into my lap!

જી   જી   ભ   જી   જી

I returned to Wisconsin with mononucleosis. My throat had swollen to the size of a muskmelon. There are doctors — and then there are doctors. Doctor Glenn Smiley was the best. He was the sort of family doctor you believed to be family. But his first prescription of antibiotics had little effect. By the third week, I was so sick I could barely get out of bed. One evening, Doc Smiley knocked on my bedroom door. He had made a house-call.

"Hi," he said, "I hadn't heard from you. How're you doing?"

"Okay, oy geos." I responded as if having a mouth full of marbles.

He took one look at my throat and called our pharmacist at home. It took at least two more weeks on a different medication before I'd recover.

My life back in New York had worn me down. I had worked so hard. I had nearly six years of extensive studies, a hundred auditions and nothing to show for it but a diminished immune system. And

I'd been lonely a good deal of the time. There had been women. I had "fallen in love" several times but, having no idea what I wanted in a woman, and no way to support a family, relationships were reduced to hopeless disappointment.

As I recovered from mono, the boredom of small town life began to drive me back into my music. I hooked up with a bandleader named Mike Wolf and began playing gigs in small bars and clubs in the area. I continued to write and we recorded a couple of sides, which I intended to bring back to Hal Webbman in New York, if I decided to return. Deciding was the hard part.

Now, I have mentioned God many times in previous pages. Though I had converted with my mother to Episcopalian and sung in the choir through my high school years, I was anything but a "believer." I had always *felt* there was a higher being, possibly, a "creator." An accidental universe didn't make sense to me. But "believing" to me was synonymous with blind faith, which I categorically denied. How about *reasoned* faith? Why hadn't they been preaching that? The Catholic answer of "Because it is a mystery" to every earnest but difficult question, just didn't cut it.

I had been resolved to call myself an agnostic, which meant I was bound to no formal moral code. I just coasted. If my behavior or actions caused me (or others) trouble or pain, I simply tried not to make the same mistakes again. Yet, I would pray. And I felt a sense that when I prayed, I was speaking to (and being heard by) a distinct and benevolent being. As most young people do, I dabbled in extrasensory perception, palm readings at carnivals or astrology. The Delavan High School had even hired a physic to lecture in what was referred to as a paid assembly. Peter Hercoss was making front-page news nationally with his crime-solving abilities, utilizing ESP. I found it interesting but neither organized religion nor paranormal phenomenon seemed important to my ambitions or everyday life. On the other hand, part of me was always open to the possibilities.

One night after being away from New York for almost six months, I lay in bed sleeplessly debating my choices. There came a point where the frustration over not being able to make a decision — *any* decision — became unbearable. My life had become a coin toss.

My old Bible still lay, unread for years, on my bureau. I got out of bed and slid a finger randomly between the pages. "Lord help me to decide," I prayed. I opened to the page and read the words my finger had arbitrarily selected. It read "Young men in your youth, be true to your hearts." The next morning I was on the first plane back to New York.

෨ ෨ ൪ ൰ ෨

My arms were full of grocery bags as I unlocked the door to my apartment. I had heard my phone ringing all the way down the hall. I had been away for so long, I was surprised anyone still remembered my number. As I fumbled with the key and tripped over the floor mat, I finally reached the phone on its seventh ring.

"Hello?"

"Is this Gary Burghoff?"

"Yes"

"My name is Arthur Whitelaw."

"Yes?"

"I'm a producer and I have a project I'm told you'd be perfect for."

". . . . . ."

"Mr. Burghoff? Are you there?"

"You mean an acting project?"

"Yes, it's a new musical called, *You're a Good Man Charlie Brown*, based on the Peanuts comic strip . . . You know the strip don't you?"

"Sure, doesn't everyone?"

"You see, we've been trying to track you down for months. Barbara Minkus has been signed to play Lucy and she's told us we had to find you to play the title role of Charlie Brown."

". . . . . ."

"Mr. Burghoff?"

"Yes . . . Yes, I'm here."

"It's a difficult role to cast. We're auditioning a few actors in the morning. Can you be at Theater 80 Saint Marks at 11:00 a.m.? If Barbara is right, you may be our man."

"Why did Barbara think I was right for it?"

"She said something about you being so kind hearted, you hired the handicapped as your audition pianists. See you tomorrow."

Click . . . Buzzzzz.

Let's do another Mrs. Heffernan.

About seven months earlier, Barbara Minkus and I, along with a dozen others, were chosen by *The CBS Repertory Workshop*, a Sunday morning TV show, which showcased aspiring and talented newcomers. It was a onetime appearance comprised of young talent who, though jobless, had made an impression on producers and directors who had auditioned them around town. It aired once and then evaporated. It had made it possible for me to join AFTRA (American Federation of Television and Radio Artists) union, though. At the end of the television season, all the actors and variety performers who had appeared in the series were brought back for a live stage review to be performed at a high society night spot called the Roosevelt Grill. The audience was comprised of invited producers, directors and agents. I arrived at the Roosevelt Grill to rehearse my song, "You're Gonna Hear from Me," at noon on the day we were to perform. There was limited time to rehearse and when my turn came along I handed my musical arrangement to the three house musicians who would be my accompanists for the 8 p.m. performance.

Now by this time, after playing in jazz bands in town, hanging around rock and roll-oriented Tin Pan Alley and studying in Charles' musical theater class, my musical style was a mishmash. Tony Bennett was my favorite singer, however, and I loved the slow, persistent 4-beat-jazz-feel he incorporated into his ballads. It was the feel I hoped the trio at the Roosevelt could accomplish. They couldn't. They were society musicians who played what Jazz musicians called "2 Beat" or "Mickey Mouse music." Halfway through my ten-minute rehearsal, I realized I was sunk. I stopped the rehearsal and asked the producer if he could rehearse someone else to give me a little time to call my own accompanist. I had no jazz accompanist!

In desperation, I phoned a friend at a music publishing company for help in tracking one down. I had minutes to accomplish it. I dropped a quarter in the payphone in the lobby and dialed her number.

"Bonnie, Is that you?"

"Hi, Gary; what's up?"

"Listen, I'm in deep trouble. I need a really good accompanist over at the Roosevelt Grill — one who understands that Tony

Bennett jazz feel, and I need him in thirty minutes."

"Gary, you stay right there. I'll send the best accompanist in New York." *Click . . . Buzzzzz.*

I went back up to the rehearsal and waited not really believing that she could track down anyone in thirty minutes. But in twenty-nine minutes, the doors flung open and in walked a blind man and his seeing-eyed dog!

Oh, God, I begged. This couldn't be . . . I mean . . . I've got a *written* arrangement!

In a thick Scottish brogue, this robust, red-haired man shouted, "Is therrree a Garrry Burrrghoff here!?"

"Uh . . . yes . . . over here!" I responded.

The dog, hearing my reply, turned immediately and led him directly to me. (Now, I'm sure that readers of autobiographies suspect that authors are prone, now and then, to exaggeration or at least "literary license," but I swear that every word is true.) As he held out his hand he said, "Hello, me name is Joel Shulman. What nuumber aire ye' doin?"

"'You're Gonna Hear from Me' . . . but . . ."

"Do ye' do it in "G" with the key change to E-flat at the last eight bars?"

I was flabbergasted. "Why, yes, I do, but . . ."

"Cumon, we got werrrk to do."

His dog led him to the piano and, as if he had done it a thousand times, lay down next to him as he sat. Shulman played a perfect eight-bar introduction (in a Tony Bennett 4-beat-style), and supported, even *inspired* me all the way through. Bonnie was right! This guy was the best accompanist in New York! He not only inspired my performance that night, I hired him to play all my auditions thereafter.

Back to Arthur's phone call.

What the hell was going on here? I had just hung up the phone having talked to what sounded like a bona fide producer, offering me the chance of a lifetime, because I had been recommended by a friend who thought I was kind hearted, because I hired the handicapped! Joel Shulman wasn't handicapped. His blindness had made him the most sensitive and brilliant musician in New York. And I had no idea he was blind in the first place! But Barbara

Minkus had observed that rehearsal and she thought I knew, and that's all that mattered.

Was there an unseen force at work here?

At the time my agnostic brain couldn't fathom it. It was just some kind of "weird coincidence." Besides, after six years of struggling, I was not inclined to look a gift producer in the mouth.

Early the next morning, I stood at the corner, in the worst February snowstorm New York had seen in a hundred years, trying to hail a cab. When I finally got one, I was so heavily laden with thick layers of slushy, wet snow that I had to remove my Borgana imitation fur parka to shake it off before entering.

"I'm going to Theater 80 Saint Marks on the Lower East Side."

The driver skidded and slid his way southward at about five miles an hour all the way to the theater. I had left myself plenty of time, having not forgotten my fiasco six years earlier on my first day of acting school. The normally twenty-minute trip took an hour and fifteen minutes. It was 10:45 when I arrived.

The tiny theater on Saint Marks Place held only two hundred seats. As I entered the lobby door, my heart sank when I saw at least a dozen actors waiting to audition. Many of them looked more like Charlie Brown than the comic strip character did! One was only about 5' tall and I recognized him immediately. It was Paul Williams, the up-and-coming songwriter, who had written a multitude of hits, including one of my favorites, "We've Only Just Begun." He was very talented and I was sure he would be the one chosen to play Charlie Brown.

We all eyed each other and tried to hide our competitive instincts behind one-liners and forced laughter, which we bandied about nervously. Suddenly, it occurred to us that the power was off in the theater. We had been standing in cold semi-darkness in the lobby. We could all see our own breath. It was freezing!

A man dressed in a casual sports jacket, his collar raised to shield his neck from the cold, came out through the theater entrance curtain.

"Hello, everyone, I'm Joe Hardy, the director."

We knew who he was. He had directed several off-Broadway hits.

"We've run into a little problem. The storm has caused a power failure. We have no lights or heat in the theater or for that matter, anywhere else in New York. We hope you've dressed warmly. For the next several hours, we will all have to rough it. Our piano player has been delayed and we are trying to find a replacement so we can begin the auditions." Pulling his jacket collar closer to his neck, he continued: "You will not be expected to sing the usual razzle-dazzle show tunes; 'Happy Birthday' or 'Twinkle, Twinkle, Little Star' would be fine. You will be playing the essence of childhood and innocence. We hope to begin in a few minutes." He disappeared into the dark theater.

One by one we were called onto the stage, which by this time had been lit by flashlights and candles. Backstage, we could barely hear the others as they auditioned. Evidently, they had found a replacement piano player. The sound of piano accompaniment was about all we heard. I was the last to be called.

As I walked onstage, I was still wearing my heavy imitation fur jacket, complete with hooded parka. I looked like an Eskimo! To break the ice (literally), I shot off the one-liner "You sure Sonja Henie started like this?"

Joe Hardy yelped out a laugh in the fourth row. "What would you like to sing?" he asked.

I walked over to the side where the "replacement" piano player sat. He was dressed smartly in a three-piece, pin-striped suit. "Just play 'Over the Rainbow' and relax. They probably don't know what they want, anyway," I whispered.

"I'm sure they don't," he whispered back.

I sang the famous Judy Garland classic as simply and wistfully as I could and left the stage.

"Thank you," Hardy said. "Please wait backstage."

When I got offstage, a man who looked like a stage manager, said "Wasn't that nice of Mr. Whitelaw to sit in on the piano at his own auditions?"

The "replacement" was the PRODUCER! I had just told him he was probably an idiot! *So long, big break.*

I had a sudden vision of the black patent-leather briefcase I would carry as my father's sales rep. Though I waited as asked, I was sure I had blown it. Then a strange feeling came over me. Here we all were in these ridiculous, even hilarious circumstances; I had just blown my chance of the century, why not just relax and have some

fun with it? Suddenly, I was enjoying myself. All the tension of
the whole last six years seemed to melt away with the snow off my
still-dripping parka.

When they called us back onstage, there were only five of us left.
I was sure they had only kept me to be polite, but I was loose and
having a ball.

Joe Hardy came down to the stage and said, "We are going to play
a little game. When I say 'mill,' I want you all to just mill around
until I say STOP. Then I want you to just start up a conversation
with the person standing closest to you."

Okay, I thought, I can mill, and if my lips aren't completely
frozen when he says stop, I can probably talk.

"MILL!" he shouted.

We walked around the stage feeling as though we were in grammar
school, playing musical chairs. In about twenty seconds, he yelled,
"STOP!" As I said, there were five of us. That's an odd number. I
had wondered off to one side. There was no one near me. The other
four actors began conversing, as directed. I was all alone. So I just
started talking to myself. "Wouldn't you know it," I said softly,
"I wait my whole life for a chance like this, and God sends a
snowstorm; I mean . . . this is GOD I'm talking about. Even if I
could afford a lawyer . . . whom do I sue?"

I was aware that Arthur Whitelaw, now sitting in the second row,
laughed and slapped his knee simultaneously. Joe Hardy leaned over
to him and in an excited whisper, loud enough for us to hear,
exclaimed, "We've found him! *That's our Charlie Brown!*"

I was hoping they meant *me*, but I refused to believe it.

We were all politely thanked and I snow-shoed myself twenty
blocks uptown 'til I was able to hail another cab home. A few minutes
after, I returned to the sanctity of my tiny studio apartment, where
I was heating water to make an instant hot chocolate, the phone
rang. The voice on the line sounded vaguely like that of the man I
had assumed was the stage manager back at the theater.

"Mr. Burghoff?"

"Yes."

"I'm calling to ask your *sizes*."

"My . . . *what?*"

"Your sizes . . . you know . . . shoe sizes, shirts, sweater, pants."

"Why would you . . . what are you *saying?*"

"You mean they haven't called you?"

"*Who?* I just got in."

"Mr. Whitelaw and Mr. Hardy . . . *You're going to be Charlie Brown!*"

Peanuts creator Charles Schulz provided this commentary for the Original Cast Recording. © KING FEATURES SYNDICATE, INC. ALL RIGHTS RESERVED.

CHAPTER 10

Cℛ

Now just about everyone in New York, and I mean EVERYONE, thought it couldn't be done . . . Everyone, except Arthur Whitelaw, Gene Person (his co-producer), Joe Hardy, and their little troop of talented hopefuls.

What Joe Hardy knew that everyone else didn't, was that playing little kids required fully trained ACTORS who understood how to play the ESSENCE of innocence. This meant avoiding the obvious trap of playing little children from a cynical and jaded adult perspective. If you made that fatal mistake, you would appear coy and cute, taking attention away from the greater values of human first discovery, disappointment and ambition. Those qualities were *universal.* Everyone understood them and would value greatly being transported back in time to their own precarious and innocent beginnings.

We had no script. That's right, I said, *no script.* What we did have was a perfect set of songs written by the sensitive and talented Clark Gesner, which captured poignantly the qualities and situations inspired by Charles Schulz's internationally beloved *Peanuts* comic strip.

The miracle Joe Hardy had to perform was tying those songs together with scenes and vignettes from Shultz's actual comic strip material. So, on the first day of rehearsal, instead of a script, we were handed volumes of actual strips, which had been previously published. Not one word would be added, not one phrase ad-libbed. If Schulz hadn't written it, we wouldn't say it.

We then, as a team, began to select our favorite strips and we would begin, moment to moment, to live them on the stage. Joe never blocked a scene (meaning he never told us when or where to move). We found our own blocking naturally and organically motivated by our emotional instincts.

Pat Berch was brought in to embellish some of the movements we had originated into simulated dance for the musical numbers.

Scenes and songs were switched around as we added new strip material we had discovered. Through Joe's watchful eye, we began to organize them into an order, which approximated a story line that turned out to be a day in the life of Charlie Brown.

Even the lighting, which was designed at the last minute before we opened for previews, was designed in the essence of color, shape, and form by rear projection.

And our set pieces also were made to simulate — abstractly — children's building blocks, which were multi-functional to suggest Snoopy's doghouse, a seesaw, Charlie Brown's baseball diamond or Schroeder's piano. The audience would fill in all the rest with their own active imaginations. We were creating visual radio; first discovery in the mind's and heart's eye.

When we opened the night of March 7, 1967, the critics entered the little theater thoroughly prepared to pan the production. One, from the *Daily News*, it was rumored, had actually written his negative review *before* he came to the opening! He was escorted out during intermission, drunk as a roach in a wine jug and was deposited into a cab. The *Daily News* was printing his devastating review, even before the second act curtain had risen. But *the others* — the big three, Nadel from the *Tribune*, Watts from the *Post*, and most of all, Walter Kerr from the *New York Times*, raved: "Run, don't walk to "Charlie Brown" at Theater 80 Saint Marks! He's got the best small combo in town!" Kerr wrote, along with his full-page rave review. He even went so far as to invite other actors, directors and producers from way up on Broadway to come see us and learn how a musical *should* be done!

Every night, in that tiny theater, I would fight to keep my concentration, after glimpsing across the footlights, legends like Judy Garland, Burt Lancaster, Paul Ford, Composer Richard Rodgers and film director Otto Preminger — all who came to see US.

One morning I received a call from Mr. Preminger's office at the Columbia Building: "Mr. Preminger would like to know if you would be willing to discuss participation in his future films." His personal secretary said.

I wanted to shout "YEEHAHOO!" but I felt "Sure, how about tomorrow at two?" more appropriate.

It was film. That's what I ultimately wanted. It was having the privilege of an audience's sole attention for two and half-hours in the dark, which lured me. That's where you could communicate and connect with the world. That's when the world became *family*.

Otto Preminger had his own floor at the top of the Columbia Building. As the elevator opened, I looked right, then left. The hall seemed to extend a mile! To my right, a handsome young man opened a door at the end of the hall.

"Mr. Burghoff, this way please. Mr. Preminger is waiting."

Do you remember the scene from Charlie Chaplin's masterpiece *The Great Dictator*, when Hynkel interviews Napoloni in Hynkel's private office? Hynkel had shortened the legs on Napoloni's chair to make him appear and feel smaller, and less significant? Although Mr. Preminger had not hired a carpenter, that's the way I felt sitting before him at his huge and tastefully appointed desk. We discussed several new films he was planning, which included one in which he planned to introduce Liza Minelli, which I knew I was perfect for. When I left his office, for the first time in six and half years of auditioning, I felt sure he would hire me and I would soon be on my way to motion picture stardom . . . NOTHING! Weeks and months went by — no call from Preminger. The trade papers were full of news about Liza's debut film and her newly discovered co-star, Wendell Burton.

What had I done wrong at the interview? Did I seem too inexperienced? Did my demeanor project insecurity? Or was there really a GOD who loved me and in his wisdom, was waiting to grant *what I needed?*

"HAIL TO THE CHIEF"

Hail to the Chief
The Colonel did elect him
'Cause he took the Major's orders
And shoved them up his nose.

— SONG PARODY BY GARY BURGHOFF
M*A*S*H FEATURE OUTTAKES
1969

CHAPTER 11

CR

Bill Hinnant was not only one of the best actors I had ever seen, he was one of the best human beings. He was our original Snoopy in *Charlie Brown*. There was also his brother, Skip (Schroeder), Karen Johnson (Patty), and Bob Balaban (Linus). And then, there was Reva Rose! Reva *was* Lucy! My benefactor, Barbara Minkus, quit before rehearsals began to accept the "better offer" of a Broadway show up town. Reva Rose was one of those excellent actresses who subconsciously became the character on and (unfortunately) offstage.

About two weeks into the run, Gary Burghoff's relationship with Reva Rose, my respected cast mate, began to morph into Lucy-versus-Charlie Brown backstage. She was constantly critical of everything I'd say or do. She laughed at the way I dressed, acted smugly indifferent to a scene or song I had just performed, and one night she even stormed into my private dressing room (privately shared with my three male co-stars) and began knocking my makeup off my shelf!

"Look how sloppy you are! Your makeup table is like a pigpen!"

If you have been living on Mars and you don't remember Lucy's relationship with Charlie Brown in the comic strip, I've just described it.

In the beginning of rehearsals, she was sweet, hardworking and affable but, as she slowly became Lucy during the run, she related to each of her fellow actors as Lucy related to her comic-strip cohorts. That meant I was **it**!

One night, two of her actor friends came to see the show and dropped in backstage. They had both worked with her in a long run in summer stock. Discreetly, I took them both aside to ask, "When you worked with Reva, was she easy to work with?"

"Reva?" they responded. "Reva is the kindest, sweetest, most benevolent person in the world."

Then I asked, "Did you know her apart from the play you were in?"

They thought for a moment before responding, "No, we met her at rehearsals and haven't seen her since we closed."

"What character did she play?" I asked.

"She played a nun," was their answer. Suddenly I knew I was in deep shit for the rest of the New York run!

Bill Hinnant was just the opposite. Not only was his performance of Snoopy inspired — so was his life. He was warm, funny, kind and wise, extremely intelligent, and well read. Socially, he was enthusiastic and loyal to his friends. I counted him among the few best friends I'd ever had. Skip was a joy. Karen was a lover. And then . . . Bob Balaban! Bob, whom you now know for his excellent motion picture character acting in such noted films as Steven Spielberg's *Close Encounter of the Third Kind*, early on in *Charlie Brown* began to "steal" the show. When we first opened, he played "Linus" professionally and competently. By the third week of performances, he had grown in confidence and full understanding of, not only his character, but where all his laughs were and all of us who had scenes with him had to be on our toes to "hold our own" against his totally charming performances. I remember admiring his rapid growth as an actor.

Throughout the year, *Charlie Brown* continued to win awards and charm New York audiences. My parents flew in from Wisconsin to see it. I couldn't resist breaking my professional concentration while onstage now and then, to observe my Father's reaction. He, like all our audiences, was grinning ear to ear, not only because he was enjoying the entirely winning material and performances, but also, because he was relieved at my "overnight success" and because he was proud. And, I assumed, because I had not become a "Chorus Boy."

Toward the end of our first year, there was a rumor going around that our producers were planning a Los Angeles *Charlie Brown* Company. I had achieved excellent attention in Ed Sullivan's national newspaper column as well as such coast-to-coast TV programs as *The Today Show*. I went to Arthur Whitelaw's office to beg him and Gene Person to allow me to help them in L.A. by recreating my performance there. They agreed! And my salary in L.A. would more than triple (from the $65 they had been paying to a whopping $250 per week)!

Though I was sad over leaving my fellow cast members (even Reva) behind, Hollywood was still my chosen destination and the opportunity might never again present itself. I was *finally on my way.*

$$\text{\small ∿ \quad ∿ \quad ☪ \quad ∾ \quad ∿}$$

When I rented my one-bedroom guesthouse in the Hollywood Hills and night fell, I had a view of the lights of the Hollywood valley below that rivaled the heavens. My Hollywood pad was out of a dream. It was one enormous living- kitchen- and dining-area adjoining a large master bedroom and bath. It overlooked a beautiful kidney-shaped, lighted swimming pool. My landlords lived on the upper level of the house and I had my own double entrances, which gave me total privacy. After six years of cramped quarters back in New York, I thought I had died and gone to, well, Hollywood.

In addition to my salary from *Charlie Brown*, my agents at the Ashley Famous Talent Agency were getting me television commercials, which nicely supplemented my meager income. I was working my way up to an enviable IRS audit!

And like my first day in New York, when the immensity of the famous West Coast City was overwhelming me, I looked out my window to view my new neighbor on his patio across the street. It was Charles Nelson Reilly, my kind and generous teacher from New York! Charles had also just moved to Hollywood to begin work on the Twentieth Century-Fox TV series, *The Ghost and Mrs. Muir.*

This world was getting smaller by the minute.

I remember thinking "*Is this all coincidence* — or what?" I was to learn, little by little, it was "or what." But at the time, I just accepted my life as the way things fortunately were.

So, I began rehearsal at the Ivar Theater, again under Joe Hardy's masterful direction. My new cast included Judy Kaye as "Lucy" (she didn't take her character home) but she was destined for Broadway stardom! We opened in the 300-seat theater before a star-studded audience and the rave reviews rivaled those of New York. *Charlie Brown* would run for two years breaking the all-time Los Angeles Theater record!

One of my agents at Ashley Famous was a man named Mark Harris. One afternoon before I left for the theater, he phoned to say, "Gary, tomorrow I want you to meet me at the Fox Studio. I've gotten you a pass. There's an independent film being planned to be shot on the backlot. I think they are interested in you for one of the parts."

"What's the title of the film?"

"It's called *M*A*S*H*.*"

"What's it about, potatoes?" I asked.

"No, it has something to do with medics in the Korean War. The director, Robert Altman, has been doing some interesting work. But you will be meeting with the producer tomorrow afternoon at one."

Now, the chance of being hired to do *any* motion picture was the answer to my life's dream. If he had told me the film was about high colonics in a health spa, I would have jumped at the chance to audition. But, a film being shot on the backlot sounded like a little independent production and the strange *M*A*S*H* title didn't impress me. I had no idea who Altman was, and I forgot to ask the name of the producer.

Consequently, as I drove my newly acquired '59 Chevy Impala through the gates of Twentieth Century-Fox Studios the next afternoon, I was relaxed, cheerful, and not expecting anything of much importance to happen. Mark met me just outside the guard's booth and escorted me to the producer's bungalow. On the door hung a plaque, which simply read "Ingo Preminger." *Preminger?* I thought. Sounds vaguely familiar.

We waited in his outer office for about thirty seconds, when his voice beckoned from within.

"Meester Harris, comb in! Comb in!"

As we entered, there standing behind his desk, grinning as he saw me and speaking in a thick Austrian accent, was a tall, fortyish, salt and peppered haired man, who looked at me as if he had seen me before and was glad to see me again. I still had no idea who he was.

"Hello, Meester Burghoff! Please have a seat!"

We sat, exchanged a few pleasantries concerning how nice the weather was and how happy he was for my success in *Charlie Brown*. The whole thing lasted two minutes. Then he rose, extended his hand and said, "Okay . . . Veerry Guud! You go now!"

As I left, I turned once to see him still grinning as if in total delight that he had seen me "again." This wasn't an audition. It wasn't even a job interview. It was a short visit with an "acquaintance" whom I'd never met. Yet there was something entirely likable about him and . . . his name was very familiar. I viewed the entire encounter akin to bumping into a mild acquaintance while on a sightseeing tour through the great Twentieth Century-Fox Studios.

Soon after I got home, the phone rang. It was Mark.

"You do want to be in the movies, don't you?" he teasingly asked.

"Of course."

"You got the part!" He said.

"What part?!"

"You'll be playing a character named "Radar." I'm having the script sent over to you now."

"Great! Are they paying me?"

"How does $10,000 sound?"

Now at the time, it sounded too good to be true.

"Mark, that's fantastic . . . Say, who is Ingo Preminger, anyway?"

"Don't you know? He's Otto's little brother."

No wonder I didn't have to audition! Otto Preminger, God bless him, hadn't forgotten me after all! He had recommended me to his brother Ingo, and they had, in advance, chosen me to play the role! All Ingo needed to see was that I could still walk and talk. It was the easiest job I had landed in seven long years. It would also be the most important of my life.

I had to ask Arthur for an eleven-week absence from *Charlie Brown*. Fortunately, knowing he was underpaying me, made it impossible for him to disagree, and my understudy had been well prepared.

The *M*A*S*H* script by Ring Lardner, Jr., turned out to be intriguing and well written. I had a meeting with Robert Altman in his office at Fox, which turned out to be even shorter than the one with Ingo. All he asked me was, "What color do you see Radar's hair?"

"Dark," was my astute, professional answer.

He seemed satisfied and I went home to study my script.

The script for the film had followed the novel, which had been written by Richard Hooker. The book began with the words "When Radar O'Reilly, just out of high school, left Ottumwa, Iowa, and enlisted in the United States Army . . ." signaling that my character played an important part as the glue, which connected the storyline. Although, Hooker's moderately successful book had been written in novel form, it was actually his true account of his Korean War experiences. Suddenly, the project took on meaning for me. After John F. Kennedy's murder, we had become seriously entangled in Vietnam. The death counts of our fellow citizens in our Armed Forces, delivered nightly on the evening news, were heart wrenching. Like many young Americans, I was having serious second thoughts about the wisdom of our involvement in a war in which we seemed to lack the resolve to win. In fact, it forced almost everyone to focus on the folly of war in general.

The M*A*S*H script promised to be an entertaining, irreverent dark comedy, which possessed the dual qualities of being entertaining and deeply poignant, simultaneously. That was the mark, I thought, of an important piece.

For the actors, the first day of production was always dedicated to the selecting of wardrobe. I reported to the Fox lot at 9 a.m. and the gate guard directed me to the wardrobe department. Now, a schooled actor has learned two basic ways to become his character: from the outside-in or from the inside-out. Sometimes a character is written so emotionally and experientially close to you, you are able to internally feel him meld with you immediately. But, "Radar" was a mystery. He hardly said much, except when he had to and there was little of his background or inner life described in either the novel or the screenplay. I had to hope that I could "flesh him out" from the outside in.

My wardrobe man, John Engtlehoffer, was a veteran of Hollywood's Golden Age. He was a kind and experienced man and had dealt with every actor from Clark Gable to the humblest extra. He was over 70, yet he still maintained enthusiasm. When I asked him if I could select my own costume, he readily agreed to "suggest" rather than "insist." He handed me an army helmet from the correct period. Inside was a knit cap.

"What's that?" I asked.

"It's a helmet liner."

I removed it from the steel helmet and put it on. It had a non-regulation look. Was Radar a little rebellious in the face of authority? Or was he just too busy doing what had to be done to pay attention to authority? I kept the cap. Next, John handed me a pair of period army boots.

"Oh wait, these are too big," he said.

"No, that's okay, let me try them on."

They were just large and heavy enough to make me feel as though I was dragging the world around with me and they affected my walk. They probably would hurt a little, too.

"Let me keep these, John, and make the T-shirts and jackets a little oversized, too . . . Oh, and pick ones that are stained and wrinkled. He shouldn't look regulation." As I dressed and stood before the dusty, old full-length mirror, I saw a lonely little figure, which I had empathy for. That was good. He was the kind of guy almost nobody noticed; who hardly noticed himself or the way he dressed. He had more going on inside than outside.

Now the script hinted at ESP, but in the early 1950s, the period of the piece, the term was all but unknown. If Radar had "the gift," he wouldn't even have known it. Besides, you can't act ESP. It is not an action or an emotion. So how could I justify the author's intent? Something was missing. I thought of Joel Shulman. Though very talented at birth, his blindness had demanded "compensation" to achieve his desired goal. Hooker and Lardner had "Radar" anticipating the arrival of the choppers and even the Colonel's commands. He was a step ahead of everyone. Why did he sense the choppers before his cohorts?

"Hey, John, you got any period eyeglasses?"

He produced a large tray of military regulation eyeglasses. I tried several and finally found a pair just large and round enough to allow eye expression to register on camera. We removed the lenses so as not to interfere with production due to light reflection.

Now, I had him.

It was simple. The poor guy couldn't see! He could have been legally blind. That's why his other senses were more acute. Now, I could make ESP *ACTIVE*. That's working from the outside in. As with all acting, it's a process or method.

Now things began to happen inside. There was an isolation to him. He couldn't see the ball at neighborhood ball games. He didn't play with the other kids. He had become a "loner," yet, he was not selfish. Instead of joining, in his humility, he led the way.

I allowed my mind to see "Radar" at home with his family as a boy. Suddenly there was a violent storm! They needed to go to the storm cellar! The lights go out! They have seconds! But they are disoriented by the darkness. Suddenly, "Radar" (he would have to have a Christian name) grabs his mother's hand and directs everyone to hold hands as he leads them all to the cellar door and safety. When the lights go out, the blind see. This little "nobody" could be heroic.

Process — preparation — the method.

That's what the method is. It gets a lot of bad rap by people (even other actors) who don't know the first thing about it. The process brings you freedom when, finally, the curtain goes up or the camera rolls. You make REAL seem effortless, because the work has been done beforehand.

Robert Altman was an actor's dream director. He loved actors. In fact, while shooting the feature, I saw nearly everyone from the actors to the caterer make suggestions to Bob and he always listened. If an idea was naive, or not on a high level, he would offer a quick intelligent explanation as to why he didn't think it would work — BUT — he always did so in a way which encouraged us to *think — grow — and continue offering suggestions.* He was glad we, as creative people, were born. Some of our suggestions worked, and if Bob had not thought of it himself — instead of being intimidated — he was grateful that a higher value had been found. We all knew the work was about being as excellent as we could in serving the material. It was not about individual ego.

Ring Lardner's ego would be challenged. He had written a very good script but we were going for a realism that would transcend the typical war picture experience. We wanted to **be** these people.

By the time we were shooting the scene in the "swamp" where Elliott Gould's character "Trapper" enters the story, Donald Sutherland (Hawkeye), Elliott, and Tom Skerritt's "Duke" were finding the stiffness of Lardner's dialogue difficult. There was a "reality" missing. Altman immediately sensed the problem.

Remembering his own military experiences (everyone talking at once with freewheeling, overlapping, often urgent conversation), he made a fateful snap decision that he would allow us to improvise the dialogue, but we had to follow the intent of the author and the structure of his scenes. There is no freedom without discipline. The final result, though I'm sure a nightmare in the post-production editing room, was a spontaneous freewheeling and overlapping delivery where some real organic human moments emerged.

The irony of this would be that (though *M*A*S*H* would be nominated for several academy awards, including Best Director) Ring Lardner would be the only winner for Best Screenplay — without one word of his dialogue having remained in the film!

We were shooting on the Fox Ranch in the Santa Monica Mountains in Malibu. We were miles from the nearest paved roads. When I wasn't involved in a scene, I began to feel I was in summer camp. While Sally Kellerman's "Hot Lips" was busting into Colonel Blake's tent and screaming her head off about resigning her commission, I was half a mile down a mountain stream, searching for quartz crystals. You could hear her all the way to L.A.!

One shooting day, Bob Altman entered one of the hot olive-drab tents, where most of us were practicing poker (we had to learn from hired professional players; we had several poker scenes), he interrupted us saying, "Look guys, we're setting up for Sally's first nude scene where the shower curtain comes down. She's a little nervous about it. I'm only using a skeleton crew to shoot it. Please stay in the tent, I don't want to spook her with people wandering around."

I said, "Hell, if she's nervous about being nude, why don't we *all* take off our clothes? When the curtain comes down and she sees us there, she will feel right at home."

I was only half kidding, but Altman took me up on it! On the first take, when the shower curtain fell, Sally was not reacting to her fellow military medical crew in full dress sitting there applauding. What she was actually reacting to was "Radar" standing next to the camera wearing nothing but his glasses and his fuzzy knit cap! Her reaction was a little out of character, so we tried it again. The second time, *everybody* was naked. To some this may seem a little crazy, but the laughter which ensued, totally eased Sally's tension and the scene turned out wonderfully.

While always maintaining artistic discipline, Altman made moviemaking fun. He was spoiling us. Those of us who never worked with him again, longed to.

In the summer of 1969, we were ready to debut the film. We opened simultaneously in L.A. and New York. On the afternoon before the premiere, I phoned the theater in Westwood and asked to speak to the manager.

"Hi, this is Gary Burghoff, one of the actors in *M*A*S*H*, which opens in your theater tonight. Which door do the cast members enter the theater from?" I was thinking like a stage actor, who always entered by the private stage door in the alley.

"Come on, Burghoff." (He sounded annoyed) "You should know this business well enough to know that you stand in line like everybody else!" And he hung up!

To say the least, I felt rejected. *Stand in line for my own movie debut?* Whatever happened to the red carpet you always see in the Grauman's Chinese Theater scenes!? Still mortified, I jumped into my brand new Datsun two-door sedan and zipped over to Westwood. *Stand in line; what was the world coming . . .* THE LINE EXTENDED TWICE AROUND THE BLOCK! It took me fifteen minutes to find a parking place! Across the street was our competition. It was also the debut of Mike Nichols' blockbuster anti-war film, *Catch-22*, which cost over twenty-two million to produce and featured an all-star cast . . . *no line.*

*M*A*S*H* had only cost three million and we were all largely unknown. Looking back, it was the spirit of our film which made the difference. *Catch-22* was an indictment of the horror and insanity of war and was, though a dark comedy like *M*A*S*H*, a nightmarish, violent downer. *M*A*S*H* on the other hand, at its heart, was about the triumph of the human spirit. The American audience flocked to the positive.

I took my place in line. *At least my ticket was complimentary.* Just at the point when my humiliation was peaking, I heard a familiar voice from about eight people in front of me. It was Robert Altman. He was also in line — to see his own masterpiece. I was suddenly honored to wait my turn.

   ∿   ∿   &#x08;   ∿   ∿

I returned to *Charlie Brown* with a true blockbuster American original under my belt. *M*A*S*H* would gross over a hundred and ten million at the box office, a record at the time, and (it was rumored) save Twentieth Century-Fox from bankruptcy, nearly caused by the failure of (believe it or not) *Hello Dolly!* While we were busy creating on the backlot without any studio attention, *Hello Dolly!* was occupying just about every corner of the front lot and costing a fortune! Fox had a history of this sort of thing. They have always made some truly great films, but the studio heads tended to, now and then, put all their financial "eggs" in one "basket." Throwing money at a project isn't the same as nurturing originality and talent. *Butch Cassidy and the Sundance Kid* had saved them from the disaster of *Cleopatra* a few years earlier . . . Same scenario.

Charlie Brown would be closing soon. After three years of full houses, we had exhausted our available audience. I had performed nearly one thousand performances of that wonderful character. It had established my career. I was proud, even cocky. I was *self made!* No one had done it for me. When it would come time to accepted my Academy Award, I projected, I'd thank only the one who had made the sacrifice, took the risks and paid the dues . . . *me!*

I had a big surprise coming.

"I DO BELIEVE"

I just saw the sweet Madonna
She was smokin' marijuana
And I almost didn't
Recognize her smile

And when I met Othello
He was advertising Jell-O
And spending his residuals in style

But I do believe
Yes, I do do do believe
I do believe . . . in fairies!

— REJECTED SONG LYRIC BY GARY BURGHOFF,
SUBMITTED FOR THE FILM, *B.S. I LOVE YOU*
©1970

CHAPTER 12

ᎯᎯ

W hile shooting Steven Hilliard Stern's independent film, *B.S. I Love You,* a man lost his life.

The charming little film about the hypocrisy of Madison Avenue advertising agencies was destined to receive excellent reviews in L.A. and New York and flop at the box office. I was hired to co-star with Peter Kastner, a talented but discouraged young actor who longed to be a history teacher. Halfway through the shooting, Steven and the producers had to ask him to stop badmouthing the film around town. Peter was a great guy, but he was one of those rare actors who wished he could be something else (Usually, almost always, it was the other way around). The script called for a scene in which Peter's character imagines committing suicide by jumping off San Francisco's Golden Gate Bridge. Steven and the guys, excellent at visual effect techniques, had devised a way, through correct camera angles, to safely simulate the jump. But, a stuntman hadn't been hired yet. Word got out about the scene and an independent stuntman, hungry for work, took his own film crew to San Francisco and actually jumped off the Golden Gate Bridge! He planned to present the footage to our company believing that, having already filmed the jump, we would surely pay him. He had filmed his own death.

A similar tragedy had nearly occurred in the making of *M*A*S*H* a year earlier. You know the scene in the film where two helicopters, with wounded strapped to the outer landing gear, fly from over the mountain eventually landing on the pad in the M.A.S.H. compound? Altman had me and several other actors running in between them as they landed. It was a windy day at the Fox Ranch. We had no idea who the chopper pilots were. They had just suddenly flown in an hour earlier. The cast had no idea where they had come from, what the pilots' experience was, or even if the antiquated Korean War period choppers were in good operating condition. We also had no idea Bob Altman would ask his actors to run in between the blades as they landed. There was only a few feet of clearance between them!

Now when you're working on a film, there is a trust factor that comes into play. You assume your director and producer have carefully given extensive thought to your safety. So, for the first attempt at the shot, I went along. But when Altman called "Action!" and I ran across that very windy pad toward those noisy and unstable-looking contraptions, one of the propeller blades came so close it knocked my helmet liner off my head! The shot was unsuccessful. I turned and saw Altman and the camera crew safe in a trench they had dug for themselves about forty feet away. Bob was giving orders to prepare the choppers to take off again, fly over to the distant mountains and repeat the shot. I walked over to him and said, "Bob, I'm not doing this again. I'm sorry, but it's too dangerous. There's something about the wind angle; it's creating a down draft."

Bob said, "Nah, it's safe. I've flown them myself in the Air Force. We hired pros."

"Sorry, Bob, I think you should rethink and re-plan the shot."

Now understand, this was my first picture. I was, as yet, a "nobody," standing there giving this already well-established director my advice! Or maybe I was more like Radar than any of us then realized.

Altman picked an extra that resembled me and had him put on my wardrobe. He was determined to do the shot, as planned. The shot would not be completed. As the choppers tried to take off again, only one was successful. The other could not attain altitude, tipped sideways and flew diagonally off the pad down toward a slew of extras on the dirt road below (missing them by inches) and to the rocky stream bed beyond. The blades came in contact with a tree at the stream's edge and the whole chopper instantly and violently exploded! When the smoke cleared, amidst screams and horror, there sat the chopper pilot, in dazed shock, still gripping his stick, the clear plastic cockpit dome pulverized around him.

The experienced stuntmen, (the "wounded") strapped to the side, had seen it coming and had seconds to release their straps and jump before impact. They landed, bruised and bleeding, against the river's stone bed! I ran down to offer help. As I reached the now *very real* wounded, I heard Ingo Preminger shout from above "ARE THE MEN ALL RIGHT?" Simultaneously Altman was shouting excitedly to his two camera crews, "DID YOU GET THE SHOT?"

It was my first serious lesson in the film business; a lesson about directors being so engrossed in their work that they sometimes forget about safety first.

Truly miraculously, no one had been seriously hurt. Though no bones had been broken, the stuntmen were justifiably furious. They also had sensed the danger in advance, but had not spoken out. I would refuse to ever again work with helicopters in any scene, on any project. Years later, a much greater tragedy would befall the cast of *The Twilight Zone* with the horrible and unnecessary deaths of renowned actor Vic Morrow and two innocent children in the same kind of helicopter accident.

$\wp$ $\wp$ $\wp$ $\wp$ $\wp$

After the disappointing release of *B.S. I Love You*, I was sure our good reviews would carry me on to better offers. But in Hollywood, it's the "bottom line" that rules. After the film's box-office failure, my advancing film career ended as suddenly as the impact of a crash-test dummy.

During the *M*A*S*H* shooting, I had discovered Malibu on our after-work studio bus-rides home. Out the buses' window, as we traveled, I had viewed with longing the flowing emerald hills, extending for miles downward toward the endless blue Pacific. I had met a young man named Kent Anderson on an L.A.-bound train from Chicago where I had paid a short visit to my parents in Delavan. He had told me of the little cabin for rent next door to his Malibu Cliffside home. I fell in love with it as soon as I saw it. It faced two acres of green fields, which advanced to the cliffs overlooking a private section of the Malibu white sand beach and ocean. It was a long-lost link to the natural world I traded so many years before for the concrete and asphalt environment necessary in the pursuit of my career. I rented it immediately. The aging, all-wood structure of about 1500 square feet, included a living room, kitchen and single bath downstairs and a sleeping loft with adjacent office above. The rear of the little house overlooked a small lawn, dirt access road and Pacific Coast Highway (Malibu's only link to Oxnard to the North and Santa Monica/L.A. to the South). All neighboring cliff-side, oceanview properties were of at least two and half acre parcels, adorned with charming single-family homes. The fresh salt air, the open sky and the panoramic views were liberating.

In 1970, my rent was only $200 per month, but my newly installed phone refused to ring. I was out of work for the first time in four years, and my bank account was dwindling. My two credit cards soon reached their limits and while my weekly drive to the unemployment office yielded a stipend, it was barely enough to live on, let alone pay the rent. There was, for me, nothing more fearfully uncomfortable than financial uncertainty. Yet every time my worry over the matter became almost unbearable, there in my mailbox would appear a check from ASCAP, or a residual for a replay of a forgotten TV guest appearance. And month after month, as if by "magic," I received to the penny what was needed.

Kent and his beautiful girlfriend, Helen, introduced me to flea markets held around the county. I would drive over to Topanga Canyon with a pick and shovel and dig for fossils, often finding fossilized tube worm shells and mollusks, which were tens of millions years old. I made jewelry from them, often mounting them on thin leather thongs, which could be hung around the neck. I sold them at swap meets to hippies for a dollar. As the months rolled by with no work, I feared my career was ending. Bob Altman was already on his second picture, utilizing many of the *M*A*S*H* cast members as his private film repertoire company. I was not invited to join them.

One afternoon, I answered the phone.

"Gary, its John. You remember me from Jim Tuttle's class?"

"Yes, John. How are you?"

"Not very good, I'm afraid. I know how close you and Jim have been and I have bad, well, *tragic* news really. If you can, would you sit down, please?"

His tone, alone, had knocked me off my feet and into my office chair.

"Go Ahead, John."

"Jim's beautiful wife, Jane, concerned that he didn't come home last night after class, went to his studio early this morning. Jim had left a note on the door: '*Don't come in — call the police — I've hung myself.*'

"Though John's voice was soothing and sensitive, my naive New England/Wisconsin perception of life exploded instantly into a million shattered mosaics so overwhelmingly lacerating as to cause my entire body to go numb. I was in total, disbelieving shock.

"Jim had been suffering from painful bouts with diverticulitis and the doctors could do nothing surgically for him. He was getting worn down."

In my mind, I went back to a time when I had called Jim ten months earlier during the New York *M*A*S*H* debut. I was sure he had seen it. To my disappointment, Jim said, "I didn't go."

"Jim, why not, I'm your first star pupil. I thought you'd be proud."

"I heard about the blood and violence in the film. I can't bear it."

"It's about Army doctors who save lives, Jim. There's blood, but it's about dedication to life."

Strangely, he had sounded mildly detached when he continued.

"Most of my students are only doing TV commercials for a living. Is this all I've trained you for? All I've worked for? I wanted to send you into the world as purveyors of truth, not to sell toothpaste and laundry detergents."

I had been hurt and responded defensively: "Jim, you came to *Charlie Brown*. You called it a winning experience. *M*A*S*H* is no toothpaste commercial. It's an original, social commentary masterpiece!"

"It's about *war*, Gary. . . I'm tired, now . . . I . . . have to go."

"I love you."

"Me, too . . . bye."

It was the last time I would ever speak to him. This man . . . this great man, who had become my brother, my guide to knowledge, philosophy, spiritual exploration and self-discovery. This man who had earned my trust while un-judgmentally guiding me through the expelling of my mind's dark opponents, who had lovingly and patiently awaited the birth of my painfully emergent humanity, was suddenly dead by his own hand.

"Gary? You okay?"

"I'll survive, John. But, I . . . can't talk now . . . except . . . how's Jane?"

"She's, needless to say, devastated. But, she's tougher than she looks. She'll make it."

"I'll call her in a few days, John. Give her my love."

"You bet. Hang in there."

Soon after I hung up, I found myself descending the steep, narrow cliffside path to the beach below. As I walked along, I yearned to, at least, feel the surf that now and then splashed against my ankles. But, as with my inner self, I felt nothing. I stopped. The seagull cries overhead were as somber notes in a minor key lamenting the loss of beauty and hope. Suddenly, one emotion emerged. Anger. "You poor selfish son of a-bitch!" my inner voice screamed. " I loved you more than anyone else and when you murdered yourself, you rejected me as completely as you would a fly in your fucking coffee! Didn't you know you would be destroying me? Stealing back all the gifts of love you had given, wiping out all the growth we struggled together to gain? You stupid, hypocritical phony! I hate you!"

The tears came and lasted on and off for a week. Eventually, I'd forgive him, realizing my anger toward him was a transference of my guilt over feeling that I had not realized the seriousness of his depression. If only I had been less selfish, less self-centered when I last spoke to him. If only I had been sensitive enough to realize the danger. I could have helped him through it, the way he helped me through the dark a thousand times. The mourning process led me to acceptance and gladness that God had brought us together so many years before.

God. In the face of the worst tragedy of my young life, I believed. I thought about my reoccurring dream, which had left me euphoric so often as a child; the dream and euphoria I had not experienced in twenty years. Suddenly, I realized the symbolism behind my euphoria. In a flash from above, a small window shade lifted, displaying a tiny glimpse of my spiritual yearning: the meaning of my dream revealed. The symbolism which my five-year-old mind had synthesized from a Sunday school lesson; wisdom from my brother, David. Not my brother in Connecticut, whose bedroom I had shared, but my brother David from the Old Testament. My dreams "new spring grass" and its "placid pool of water" was my young subconscious minds rendering of "The Lord is My Shepherd, I Shall Not Want, He Maketh Me to Lie Down in Green Pastures, He Leadeth Me Beside the Still Waters . . ."

"SUNKEN GARDEN"

An angry neurotic named Mike
Decided to visit a psych!

At a hundred an hour
He hoped he would flower

But, then as he peddled his bike

A bump in the road sent him flying
Toward a place where he soon may lay dying

But, his landing was softened
Which happens quite often

By the wings of an angel fly-bying!

He opened his eyes in a garden
Thanked God for miraculous pardon

But within a few hours
Forgot all the flowers

His heart still resolving to harden

When he entered his therapist's womb-room
It soon became their private gloom-room

Psychological knowledge
From Freudian College

Threaten to make it his doom — room!

But, while peddling home, he delayed there
By the spot he was earlier splayed there

His body's compression
Had left an impression

In roses and daisies, displayed there.

The place where he rudely was tossed
Had maintained his deliverance embossed

Though, he still felt un-flowered
His spirit soon towered

At the sight of a flowering cross!

— EXTENDED LIMERICK BY GARY BURGHOFF
©2006

CHAPTER 13

CR

Group therapy, while "enlightening," had been largely unsuccessful. While Eric Berns' Transactional Analysis (founded on his brilliant book, *Games People Play*) was an inspiration, its implementers lacked integrity. During my L.A. *Charlie Brown* days, I had joined Elizabeth Palm's therapy group. Twice a week for a year, I had attended meetings with other "tormented individuals" hopeful of straightening out our childhood cross transactions that had led to the corruption of our adult relationships.

While Berns' genius produced a pure and practical therapy approach, which rejected Freudian psychotherapy dominated by the unbearable weight of Freud's egoistic and non-spiritual mind, the therapists practicing "TA," as it was called, were in my experience more screwed up than most of their clients!

Palms, while always sober during group, became a lush at our dinner gatherings, which often followed our meetings. After a few too many drinks, she would begin ridiculing us and revealing personal information gained in "private" sessions with our fellow patients. While dining with her at a small La Cienaga restaurant, we all spotted the famous actor Sal Mineo, whose performances in classic films such as *Rebel without a Cause* and *Exodus* had earned him respect and dignity. He was seated with a friend in a corner booth. Palms, whose alcoholic breath would ignite at the light of a match, began loudly proclaiming her belief that famous actors were no more than "lonely, disturbed children, desperately seeking attention from a neurotic public, which would pay exorbitantly for vicarious participation in their spontaneous performances, due to the squelching of their own spontaneity by their stupid parents in childhood!"

I was hoping that Mineo, being further along as a successful film actor than I, was not close enough to hear her embarrassing fifty-cent rhetoric. As I passed his booth, while leaving, I paused to introduce myself. He politely rose and warmly acknowledged that he had seen and enjoyed one of my *Charlie Brown* performances. *Suddenly*, Elizabeth Palms (our guide to "mental wellness") stepped between us, grabbed Sal's hand, and with a grip of iron, pulled his head so close, I thought she would force him to kiss her! Instead, she said in a deep "sexy" voice, "*You don't impress me; I know what you really want from life . . .*" She then, to everyone's mortification, began sucking on his nose!

Sal tried to push her away, but the petite 68-year-old drunk's grasp was totally unbreakable! I, realizing the disaster before me, grabbed her trying to pry her loose from him! No success! Finally, she "orgasmed" and let him go! His face, which expressed astounded disbelief, was covered with Elizabeth Palms' saliva! As he reached for his napkin, attempting to recover, I tried desperately to apologize for my "friend's" bizarre behavior. What could I tell him? His politeness had already righteously turned to humiliation and anger! I, and a few others, quickly yanked Palms out the door before the police were summoned!

I would like to add here that all who knew Sal Mineo still grieved his untimely death and I in no way wish the inclusion of this true and regrettable occurrence to diminish his respected memory.

I would no longer attend group therapy.

ᔰ   ᔰ   ଓ   ᔰ   ᔰ

One overcast afternoon, while loafing on Malibu's Point Dume pier, I noticed a young boy carrying a large Pacific brown pelican. This was not something you see every day in Malibu. I stopped him to ask what he was doing.

"I found it on the beach; it's sick. I took it home, but my mom says I've got to release him." I asked if he would object if I took the bird to try to heal it. He thankfully agreed, and I brought the poor, weak creature home. I phoned a local veterinarian to ask his advice. He told me that if I brought the bird to Frank Todd, who was curator of birds at the Los Angeles Zoo, he could help.

I had bought an old International Harvester milk truck, which was now my only form of transportation and which served nicely as an "ambulance." It would have to. In following weeks, after sending out word around Malibu that I was taking in ailing and injured animals, I would be deluged with dozens of ailing pelicans, which I would rush every few days to Frank at the Zoo, an eighty-mile trip each time.

Frank had explained that the entire species was endangered, due to a reoccurring virus that only attacked brown pelicans, on average, every fifteen years. But that was a *culling occurrence* meaning nature's way of thinning their numbers and improving their gene pool by natural selection, but *this time*, the natural cycle was serious because of the added threat from human sources. DDT, the so-called "miracle agricultural pesticide," mentioned in the mid-sixties in Rachel Carson's important book *Silent Spring* had so permeated the environment, it was, when combined with the natural illness, threatening to extinguish, not only pelicans, but all aquatic and songbirds, as well!

Proof had been gathered by biologists nationwide. One testing ground was Southern California's Channel Islands, where the pelicans nested. On one test island alone, which normally produced ten thousand offspring each year, in 1970, *only one* fledgling had survived! DDT, which, after being sprayed for years nationwide, had so permeated the soil that it washed into streams and rivers and eventually into our oceans. Having over a fifty-year half-life, the poison concentrations were picked up by plankton and micro-organisms at the bottom of the sea's food chain and transferred right up to the higher life forms! It had the effect on sea birds (all birds) of rendering their eggshells so thin and fragile that when the parent bird would sit on the eggs, they were breaking.

For two years, I would nurture, under Frank's guidance, hundreds of marine birds, while writing letters to newspapers and lobbying our representatives in Washington to outlaw the madness our use of DDT had become. *Fortunately*, in late 1970, we, who were sounding the alarm, were finally heard and Congress banned the lethal chemical. By the very next year, that same test island produced five hundred successful offspring and within five years, the survival rate was back to normal levels. This taught me a great lesson. Nature is *resilient* as long as we are willing to get out of its way.

I had been given the convenient name of "Birdman of Malibu." The 8' tall, wood and chicken wire cages and compounds that I had built in my little backyard contained a revolving patient list of not only pelicans, but raccoons, opossum, red-tail hawks and ailing members of every species of aquatic sea bird! On a daily basis, without exception, new patients were being brought to me. With Frank's help, I learned to set and bandage broken wings and legs, administer antibiotics and perform minor emergency surgery. I became so well known for my activities that an embarrassed Department of Wildlife insisted on officially licensing me.

One afternoon while tending my "hospital," I turned to see a beautiful, brown-eyed brunette standing near me on the lawn. She was looking for her lost kitten, "Ohm Dust." I knew instantly I loved her. As I have written, I'd "fallen in love" many times, but Janet was something else. Physically, she resembled Ali McGraw, an actress whose looks made me crazy. But Janet, like me, was of the earth. She was connected to the beauty of the natural world. She valued things other than money, fame or success. She valued life, tranquility, and kindness and was, like me, on a spiritual search. I fell so quickly and deeply for her, we were sleeping together in a week and engaged to be married in a month. Her family was large, warm and very active. They lived only two lots down from my cabin. I had already met her father and mother, Sid and Jane Gale, on a previous day when I took the wrong path up from the beach and accidentally (and embarrassingly) ended up in their backyard. I had liked them immediately and envied the family's closeness. All eight of them lived in their modest Malibu beachfront ranch house, built by Sid and his father in the 1940s. They had all grown up there together. Grandpa Gale was in his nineties and was still spry and sharp mentally. His sense of humor reminded me of my own grandparents. Then there were the three boys; oldest Jim, John and youngest Steve. And living in a camper in the backyard, was Jane's mother, also in her nineties. It was the family I had yearned for.

Janet had been away on that day and I had not known of her existence until "Ohm Dust" disappeared.

Overnight, I was accepted as part of their family and marriage plans were actively taking place. We met in October of 1970 and were married, in a private ceremony, at the Gales' family home on Christmas afternoon, three months later. My father and his sister (my Aunt Doris) flew out for the wedding. Mom feared flying and was unable to attend on short notice. As I said, the whole affair, from meeting to marriage was a whirlwind, and my parents weren't even told about the wedding until a week before it took place.

For our honeymoon, I had converted my old milk truck into my first RV! I bolted an antique, upholstered chair to the floor on the passenger's side, up front, next to the driver's pedestal. I insulated the bare, steel walls with foam and bolted a thin wood veneer over it to create interior walls. A Coleman ice cooler became our "kitchen" and a port-a-potty was stored under the double bed that I had constructed from 2 x 4's, plywood and a thick foam mattress. I even fashioned curtains around the windows for privacy.

After the wedding, that old stick shift, four-banger proudly putt-putted north on Pacific Coast Highway, heading for Vancouver, British Columbia. *In December!*

What were we thinking?

By the time we reached the Northern Oregon border, we had used all seven gas bottles of our Coleman portable heater and we were embracing each other, not so much in sexual ecstasy as in an attempt to survive the cold! But, our hearts were warm and our new life together fired our passionate dreams of a sunny and warmer future.

We had $900 to our name, which was the sum total of the cash given us as wedding gifts. By the time we drove onto the Vancouver Island bound ferry in Seattle, Washington, half had been spent on food and gas. Yet we made it to our destination — Salt Spring Island — and for a week, we scrimped and saved our pennies, made love, enjoyed the Northern island charm, made love some more — and began our descent Southward, again, toward home. In central Oregon, the engine of the old truck overheated and completely gave out. It was actually a blessing. A car dealership paid me $600 for what remained of our honeymoon cabin on wheels. We were down to our last $30. If we hadn't sold the truck, we wouldn't have made it home. We rented a car and scooted back toward the Southern California sunshine.

$\wp$ $\wp$ $\mathcal{CR}$ $\wp$ $\wp$

My modest spiritual awakening had revealed God's existence, but not his identity. A nameless God is a potential danger. Janet, who was independent from an organized religious background, was open to all, but leaned toward Far Eastern religious expression.

After doing what young married couples who love each other do each night, we would lie awake and share our mystical and spiritual experiences and philosophies. She introduced me to the Tabetin Book of the Dead, which I found astoundingly inspired and beautiful. While no longer agnostic, I was not yet ready to make a commitment to any religious dogma. My rebellious childhood had forged a stubborn non-joiner attitude toward society and that included organized religion. "Church" to me, was not a building filled with worshiping people. It was outdoors, under God's sky, his living creation around me. To nature, I was joined at birth. Creation? This, I now believed. My glimpse into divinity had clarified that. I knew that it was not nature that I would worship, it was the Creator of nature who was due praise. The third symbol in my dream had been the "calm, clear and very blue sky," which represented GOD watching over HIS CREATION.

I had been indoctrinated well in the religion of Darwinism. His theory of evolution was made believable for me by high school science teachers and children's science books I'd read. But, Mrs. Heffernan had taught history too well. I had a sense that when the elite and fashionable of any generation insist you "go along," they are often, in time, proven wrong. The unsinkable *Titanic*? The completely safe *Hindenburg*? Applying leeches to suck the patients' blood to cure diseases? The Salem Witch Trials? Insisting the sun revolves around a flat earth? These were all notions of elitists, who sometimes forced their beliefs on others, even under penalty of death! The "Christian" church, historically, had been no exception. For me, at this time, to believe that "Christ" was God's name would have been akin to my believing George Washington really chopped down that cherry tree. How did I know He didn't prefer being called "Buddy" or "Laverne"? My Methodist King James Bible only referred to Him as "The

Father" or as "God." "God" is a title like "President" or "Leader." It is not His name. Without knowing His true identity, I remained confused and aimless in my resolve to worship or commit. Consequently, I would stubbornly resist being religiously "correct." Only God Himself could convince me otherwise.

He was about to.

"THE CROOKED TREE"

When Bobby Wing was very young
He dreamed that he could fly
Just like the happy meadowlark
That brightened up his sky.

One morning as the sun came up
And no one was around
He climbed the cypress tree and jumped
And tumbled to the ground!

Don't cry Bobby Wing
Little crooked one
Remember a crooked tree
Keeps looking for the sun!

"It's such a shame" His mother'd say
"It's such a cryin' shame"
That from that day, he couldn't play
Poor Bobby Wing was lame.

And sometimes on a sunny day
When the lark came out to fly
She'd fondle him and softly say
As his eyes welled up to cry

Don't cry Bobby Wing
Little crooked one
Remember a crooked tree
Keeps looking for the sun!

Then upon a rainy day
She bowed her weary head
The Lord had taken him away

Her crooked boy was dead
And as she watched him bury him
And put her boy to bed
She whispered so no one could hear
And this is what she said

"Please take Bobby Wing
My little crooked one
Please take my crooked tree
And help him find the sun"

And as she stood there by his side
But before she had time to cry
A shadow crossed the grave
And she looked up in the sky

And there she saw a meadowlark
Hoverin' way up high
Happy little meadowlark
Brighten' up her sky!

And she knew her little crooked boy
With skylarks in his eye
Unhappy little broken toy
At last had learned to . . .

FLY! FLY! BOBBY WING!
Life has just begun!
I told you that a crooked tree
Would one day find the sun!

— FOLK SONG LYRIC BY GARY BURGHOFF
©1966

CHAPTER 14

CR

The *M*A*S*H* feature had been *avant-garde*. For its time, it was outrageously irreverent. The thought of a television network deciding to remold it into a TV series never crossed my mind. Accordingly, I would wait near the telephone hoping my agent, Peter Witt, would call with a film, stage play or even a commercial offer. He didn't.

Janet worked as a surgical technician in a Santa Monica Hospital and, to my slight embarrassment, was bringing home the rent money. Except for her, my life was *for the birds*. My animal rehabilitation center required commitment and I was learning valuable lessons from my patients. While on the Malibu Pier one day, I noticed how relaxed the wild gulls seemed as they perched atop the wooden handrails. They maintained a nearly perfect distance from one another and as long as the three feet or so between them was not encroached upon, they felt safe. It occurred to me, they're *maintaining distance to provide room for flight*. The open sky was their shelter from harm; their sanctuary. As long as they felt they could fly, they showed no fear of humans.

Back home in my compound, however, even those birds that had fully recovered were reluctant to fly away through the compound's open top. They had become too accustomed to the thawed herring I would feed them three times a day. They required encouragement to leave and resume their life of independence. I feared I was getting like that. *My* world had also become a "comfortable compound." I hadn't worked in so long, I had forgotten how to fly. I prayed for motivation.

The phone rang in the living room. Wiping the fish slime off my hands, I answered.

"Gary? It's Mike Belson from the Peter Witt office."

"Hello, Mike, what's up?"

"CBS and Fox are making a television series from *M*A*S*H*!"

". . . .   ."

"Gary? . . . Are you there?"

"Please tell me they want me for Radar," I begged.

"That's right, *if* you want to do television."

You must understand that in 1971 anyone who was working in film wouldn't be caught dead doing *television*, at least not under long-term contract, in a series. But for over a year I wasn't working in film. I just wasn't working.

"How long would I have to be under contract?"

"Three years."

"How much are they offering?"

"Fifteen hundred an episode, with a guarantee of twenty-two episodes a season."

My mind clicked through the math.

"That's thirty-three thousand a season." (Some actors made that much per episode!)

"Of course, once you sign, you could always renegotiate if your character *clicks*."

"You mean in the middle of a contract?"

"Sure. It's done all the time. I recommend you take the offer, and if you are successful, who knows, you could become a *valuable studio commodity*. Then they'd gladly pay more to keep you happy."

I was bluffing and trying to appear sophisticated. Of course, I'd take the job.

"Who's producing?"

"Gene Reynolds."

Now, I was sure I'd take it. Gene had been the only producer at Fox television to show an interest in me. He had produced and directed my only screen test a few years earlier, but the project was never picked up. Gene had been a child actor from Hollywood's golden era. His sensitive performance with Spencer Tracy in *Edison, the Man* had inspired me as a wide-eyed Hollywood dreamer back in my Forestville days. He also produced and directed Charles' successful series *The Ghost and Mrs. Muir*.

"Who's writing the pilot? It's going to be tricky adoption it for television. To do it right, we'll have to battle the censors."

"Gene's hired Larry Gelbart. You know him?"

Know him! He had written *A Funny Thing Happened on the Way to the Forum* on Broadway. He was brilliant *and* irreverent.

"Tell 'em I'll do it," I said.

Before hanging up, I added . . .

"Do they have a 'Hawkeye' yet?"

"They're trying to get Alan Alda, but he's hedging."

Alan had seen me in *Charlie Brown*. I had seen *his* performance in the little film, *Paper Lion* and admired the genuineness of both his acting and his personality when he dropped backstage, after my performance. I hoped Gene could talk him into it.

Suddenly, I had been given room to FLY. Out of the blue, my financial troubles had ended and I once again had an opportunity to show what I could contribute. Janet returned home from work to view "The Birdman" grinning as if he had just swallowed the cat!

"What's going on with you, Smiley?" she asked.

"I'm WORKING! We don't have to worry about the rent anymore."

"Oh. That's good."

Her understatement failed to inhibit my enthusiasm, I was on my way again doing a project I respected and a character I loved.

In my exuberance, I forgot to thank God for answering my prayer.

෧ ෧ ෬ ෭ ෧

Let's run the next seven years in *Fast Forward.*

Year One — long hours. Cold at the ranch in the morning. 105 degrees by noon. No shade. Working twelve to sixteen hour days. Some scripts poignant, some ridiculous TV fluff. Our ratings, very low . . . Sank to 55th. We feared cancellation. *I GOT MY FIRST EMMY NOMINATION.*

FAST FORWARD:

Year Two — we weren't cancelled! Off camera I was the "class entertainer" again. McLean Stevenson was funnier. Our scripts were improving. *I WAS NOMINATED FOR MY SECOND EMMY.* Our ratings were on the upswing!

STOP!

In year two of the series, there was good news! During the summer reruns, our ratings would skyrocket! During the first run, primetime airings, most of the audience watched the competition. But, the competition couldn't hold their interests twice. We could. Our scripts, overseen by the inspired genius of Larry Gelbart, were so intricate (more than one plot happening simultaneously) and so uniquely funny and dramatic, the modest audience who watched the first time would join the summer newcomers and watch again! Combined, the two groups made for a *huge market share*! No one at the network had ever seen this pattern. Network promotion had little positive effect. The American audience was discovering us on its own. America's a big country with big word of mouth! If CBS had considered canceling us, this new phenomenon was giving them pause. Meanwhile, our scripts and production organizing were becoming finely honed. Our twelve-to-sixteen-hour days, in year one, were disappearing as we figured out how to shoot a thirty-six-page script every four days . . . without nervous breakdowns!

FAST FORWARD:

Year two — Jackie Cooper came on as "guest" director. His production values were excellent, his demeanor, sometimes, cruel.

STOP!

Gene owed Jackie a favor for hiring him as a director during a lull in his career. He was now returning it during Jackie's lull. Cooper, who was gentle as "Charles Lamb"off the set, turned into a tyrant, on.

We had an aged assistant director named George who, though hardworking and conscientious, didn't move fast enough for Jackie. The poor guy was only working to reinforce his pension for retirement in a few months. Jackie demanded total silence on the set during and between shots. That was not only impossible for us M*A*S*Hers, it was destructive. The humor we shared between shots was what kept us connected and energized. It also dissolved tension.

Cooper gave George a whistle to blow if George heard a single sound while Jackie was planning a shot. Somebody made a slight sound. George didn't blow. Cooper went into a *TIRADE*!

"IF YOU CAN'T EVEN BLOW A WHISTLE, GIVE IT TO A YOUNGER MAN!" he loudly chided.

I lost respect for Cooper at that moment. He had been brought in after we had bonded. At first we were delighted to have him. His visual results in the final cuts were top notch, as far as production values were concerned. But, little by little, he began to take over the show. He hired a publicist to spread the word that he was the director of M*A*S*H, when in fact we had *many* fine directors. Then, at dailies, with Gene and Larry, he would take credit for many of the creative moments we (the actors) had contributed in order to bolster his image with the "bosses." He referred to me as "the kid," which I also resented.

One morning we showed up at 6:00 at the Fox Ranch to find that our decrepit, portable dressing rooms were unheated! It was 19 degrees! I fumbled with the thermostat and the old, dilapidated thing fell off in my hand. We were all getting sick and when you're doing a series, you can't afford to. I steamed out of the trailer, intending to make a complaint, and found McLean standing there gazing at a scene about two hundred yards downhill.

"Mac . . . there's no heat again . . ."

He directed my attention to the scene below.

Cooper, who was planning a summer scene, was using our loyal and devoted "extras" as stand-ins. He wanted to see "flesh tones" through the lens. He was indulgently making them stand there without their shirts! Jackie, of course, was snuggly adorned in a natural, fur-lined jacket.

"You think we've got it bad?" asked McLean rhetorically. "Look what he's making *them* do."

Mac was right. He was a very sensitive man and he cared deeply for others.

"I'm going down to talk to him," he said.

I stood there watching as he descended the hill. His body language spoke volumes as he spoke to Cooper. Mac was being diplomatic; asking questions rather than being demanding. Cooper would walk away a few yards, then storm back aggressively, as McLean would politely continue negotiating for his fellow workers. Finally, Cooper, shaking his head in disagreement, just walked away. Mac slowly walked over to one of our teamsters and asked to be driven off the ranch (we were not allowed to drive our own cars, in or out).

It was four miles, on dirt roads, to the nearest highway. He was gone forty-five minutes. When he returned, I asked what he had done.

"I went to the nearest pay phone," he said. "And I made a phone call to Bill Self, our Executive Producer."

Now, an "executive producer" may be your most important link to creative support and production stability or he may be just some guy collecting a percentage while resting on his laurels. Self was, in our experience, the latter.

"What did you tell him?" I asked.

"I said, 'Bill, this is McLean Stevenson. I'm disturbed by the work conditions Jackie Cooper is exacting on our fellow workers. Then I listed for about five minutes, all the cruelty I had witnessed."

"What did Self say?"

"He said, '*McLean Stevenson?* . . . From where do I know that name?'"

"That's it?"

"Yep . . . he hadn't heard a word I said."

"What did you say then?"

"I said he could find my name on my contract, which he could then shove up his insensitive ASS!"

About halfway through the third season, McLean had given notice. He would not return in the next year.

FAST FORWARD:

STOP!

In Mac's final episode, the original ending tag contained a humorous letter from Henry Blake, who had returned safely back home after his honorable discharge. Mac and I finished the shooting, as scripted, and were walking off the set to dress for our annual Christmas party. Gene and Larry, who were just entering, stopped us.

"Hey, guys," said Gene. "We have an alternative scene we've written, which we want to shoot."

Asking this of us was not just unusual, it was unique. I read the now-famous Henry Blake death scene and took McLean aside.

"Mac," I said, "If they kill you off, you can never change your mind. If you don't want me to do it, I'll refuse."

I was hoping he would have a change of heart during our six-month hiatus. Characters can always return, as if by writers' magic, unless they are killed off.

"No, I *want* you to do it. Don't you see? They are keeping their promise they made us."

He was referring to our first day of rehearsal, three years earlier. At the discussion table, Gene and Larry had promised that no matter how funny our scripts, we would use every opportunity to also show the harsh reality of war; the insane injustice and cruelty. The brave souls who actually suffered in Korea (in any war) deserved no less.

I did the scene . . . McLean left . . . *part of me went with him.*

FAST FORWARD:

Year four — No more Jackie Cooper (He had left after season 2). Loretta Swit and I love doing scenes together. Our ratings are in the Top Ten! . . . *I'M NOMINATED FOR THE FOURTH TIME, BUT STILL BEING UNDERPAID!*

STOP!

Though the *M*A*S*H* cast and crew were the finest professionals I would ever have the privilege of working with, there were inequities regarding salaries. In year three, during hiatus, my agent, noting three Emmy nominations, asked to negotiate a raise. Janet and I were vacationing in Hawaii when Gene and his associate, Burt Metcalf, phoned me at our condominium on Maui.

"Gary, are you unhappy?" asked Gene.

"No. I'm delighted. But Radar is becoming a very important character, Gene. Larry is writing some great stuff for him. I signed on for the low salary because I knew I'd have to prove myself on television. I think I've done that. Don't you?"

"How much do you want?" Burt asked.

"Jeez, guys . . . ask my agent. You know I can't represent my own value."

"How does $3,000 an episode sound?"

After thinking, I said, "I'll tell you what. I'll meet you halfway. You pay me *that*, but *I only work thirteen episodes a season.*"

"You mean you want LESS work?"

"Yep. Janet and I plan to have a baby. I want to be a Daddy. I want more time at home."

I had just weakened my position and my family's financial future! I was a horrible businessman. I should have let my agent take care of it. By the end of my final seventh year, though I would renegotiate one more time, I would be making less on *M*A*S*H* — the most popular and successful television show in history, seen by millions each week — than I would later make, per week, in a *300-seat dinner theater!*

But, Janet and I had invested in real estate. I was good at it. In the '70s, people were just discovering what I had known since childhood: WATERFRONT PROPERTY. The author's advice in *I Remember Mama* applied to real estate investment, also. We were buying *what we knew and loved.*

Our little one-bedroom beachfront condo on Maui had doubled in value in a year and we used our equity to buy another ocean-view condo. We used our equity in that, a year later, to buy a lakefront home on Lake Arrowhead in Southern California. Not long after we bought the Arrowhead property, wind from a bad storm blew over a humongous oak tree which fell on the charming, older, two-story home and nearly sliced the upper story in half. Thankfully, we were insured. The insurance paid for a complete remodeling, and when the work was completed, the house was worth more than double what we had paid just a few months before. If *M*A*S*H* was not making us wealthy, real estate was!

At home in Malibu, we had moved from our little rented cabin and purchased a large, comfortable four-bedroom ranch house on two acres at fashionable Bonsil Drive, complete with custom backyard pool, guest house and trout pond! *M*A*S*H* was financing our down payments and paying the mortgages and our appreciation compensated for my low salary.

I was not only doing "all right," I was getting downright cocky again.

FAST FORWARD:

STOP!

Now, I would like to stop fast-forwarding from here on. What happened next in my life was too traumatic, inspiring, and miraculous to pass over.

ה   ה   ಐ   ೪   ה

The fast forward life, which the *M*A*S*H* series had ignited, was while the answer to my life's dream and ambition, not the triumphant and dignified experience I had expected. Amazingly, my "sun" was located elsewhere. By mid-1977, in *M*A*S*H*'s sixth year, I was lost and foundering in darkness.

My physical symptoms were signaling that something was distressingly wrong with me; lower back pain so severe that my body was twisted like a pretzel; headaches, frequent fatigue and physical depression. The constant pain caused me to be irritable and impatient with nearly everyone from my loyal manager, Bob Crystal, my *M*A*S*H* cast members and even (most regrettably) my wife.

I had been nominated for the Emmy six times in a row. The award represented reaching the top of my profession. I had thought winning it was paramount to my happiness. Yet, when nominated in the sixth season, in my generally depressed state, and being resolved that I would never win, I elected, for the first time, not to attend the award broadcast. When the envelope was opened and the presenter read "and the winner for Best Supporting Actor in a comedy series is GARY BURGHOFF!" I was sitting alone, in the dark, on my dock at Lake Arrowhead, fishing for catfish. Not only did I not realize my life's dream of giving my own acceptance speech, but the fishing was *also lousy!*

Alan graciously accepted for me. He said, "In a way, I'm glad Gary couldn't be here tonight. It gives me the opportunity to tell you what a fine actor he is."

Notice he didn't include "and a great human being."

I had admired Alan Alda above all others. His intelligence, creative mind, his total commitment and devotion to the work, his ample sense of humor in the face of turmoil and tension, and his general kindness, were qualities I had to love. You may or may not know that Alan is the only artist who has won Emmy's in all four categories of Best Actor, Writer, Director and Producer. I watched him EARN that distinction, while working by his side on *M*A*S*H*. I've been a working actor for thirty-eight years as I write this, but I've come across no one who deserves more respect as a professional and as a man than Alan. He also had to fight his "lower angels" to overcome the pain and disillusionment of his early family life and, through his work and his choice of his wife, Arlene, he triumphed.

Yet, beginning in 1977, he also became the target of my often defensive and belligerent behavior. My frequent snits and outbursts on the set were inevitably (and instantly) followed by guilt feelings over what I'd just said or done. It was as if I were two people: one wicked, one good; both battling for dominion. But, I also was a target. Alan and some of my cast mates were also showing signs of the same distressing symptoms. My behavior made me an easy receptacle for their release of frustration and anger emanating from their own disillusionment and disappointment with studio politics, the workload and the sometimes-undignified public response to our sudden fame.

Fame. Please indulge me. I hope I don't break your bubble. If you think *fame* is what dedicated actors are striving for, you are very much mistaken. Fame is the unintended and undesirable byproduct of an actor's hard and triumphant work. It is a necessary evil in insuring that the work offers will continue, but it is a *double-edged razor*! It slices painfully and deeply into the qualities which make your essential private life worthwhile: dignity and liberty.

Out of thousands, let me share just one encounter. In *M*A*S*H*'s third season, while on hiatus on Maui, Janet and I were standing in line awaiting a table in a crowded restaurant. Until this time, our privacy had been relatively respected. Suddenly, through a corner booth curtain, to my immediate right, shot a sharp manicured forefinger, which painfully and alarmingly pierced my ribcage. "Hey, Radar!" shouted the coy, anonymous voice behind the curtain. "How come you're not in Korea?" To the "enthusiastic" woman who had just speared me, I had become her nightly TV buddy, with whom she felt totally comfortable in taking liberties. To Janet and me, it was akin to an assault by a demented stranger! Before I could even respond, her loud utterance of my character's name created a sudden frenzy from others around us. Janet was roughly pushed aside by the crowd, which pinned me against the wall! "Stand there! Let me take a picture for my Uncle Benny in Duluth," a man demanded. As soon as his fumbling fingers learned to operate the camera and the flash ignited, the others around derived immediate tacit approval to accelerate the impromptu and alarmingly disorderly photo-op! I felt the wetness of the blood from my side as it began to stream through the white shirt I had worn. I held out my hand to Janet to draw her close to me. The look on her face, to this day, is burned into my memory. It conveyed, *Is this the life your chosen career has thrust us into?* She was bewildered and hurt. *Is this the environment we will be experiencing each time we bring the baby, which grows inside me, into the world?* Part of me knew, at that moment, our life together was in jeopardy. All this because a foolish woman with a phony Hollywood fantasy of fame-protocol uttered "RADAR" in public. Though Janet and I tried desperately to deny it, at that moment, we were as a happy married couple, doomed.

She was too real, too connected to truth and natural beauty and to the spiritual search, the pursuit of which, required *tranquility*. She knew God *whispers* his wisdom and could not be heard in an environment of worldly hysteria. I loved her for the very reasons I've just listed. Yet, I felt powerless to protect her from the path FAME was persistently leading us toward. Though I had studied my art for six long years in New York, there was never a course on how to handle fame. Even Meisner and Tuttle had not experienced it. Now, I was beginning to know its true nature and had experienced only one rude and bloodied tip of many jabbing fingers to come. It was a vicious and unpredictable enemy!

At that moment, I remember being relieved that my instincts had, at least, prompted me to negotiate for less work on *M*A*S*H*. FAME would ruin my beloved *M*A*S*H* experience along with my long, yearned-for dream of a happy and loving family. It would once again hurl me off track toward abnormality and in the end . . . *nearly* kill me.

"RADAR'S LULLABY"

Bye-low baby
Bye-low baby
Bye-low baby
Bye-low baby, bye

Daddy still loves you
Daddy still loves you
Daddy still loves you . . .
Although, he's gone to war.

IMPROVISED LULLABY BY GARY BURGHOFF,
SUNG TO A KOREAN ORPHAN.
*M*A*S*H*, SEASON FOUR,
EPISODE TITLE: "THE KIDS"

CHAPTER 15

℞

My beautiful daughter Gena was born at St. Anthony's Hospital the night of July 20, 1975. From the first moment I held her in my arms, I knew she was the reason I had been born. All other dreams, ambitions and success in the work place would now only serve to provide a safe and nurturing life for her. I made the conscious and unwavering decision that I would no longer "live to work," I would rather "work to live," shifting my life's focus to my family. *M*A*S*H* was making that shift possible. At least for the next three years, I would not have the distraction of having to scratch for a living. But, the quality of my work had become an obsession to me. As each thirty-six-page script flew by during production, the pressure I put on myself to exceed my last performance became overwhelming. My intensifying focus from work to my family's welfare was counter-productive. After experiencing the insecurity of having been out of work and forgotten after *Charlie Brown*, I, like my job-oriented father before me, began pushing myself to achieve greater "excellence" in my performances. My over-perceived sense of responsibility was having a negative effect with my cast and crew relationships on the set and with Janet, at home.

From my perspective, my TV life would only last briefly. Radar's popularity would probably overshadow any other character I had played, or would ever play again. I was correct. In a very real way, my hope to become a film actor had already ended. But if I could, in the few seasons left on *M*A*S*H*, I'd leave an impression with the industry so brilliant and impressive that work offers from film producers *might* come in. Steve McQueen, who graduated from TV's

The Bounty Hunter to a flourishing film career, had proved it, though rarely achieved, possible. I had become the worst sort of perfectionist and though I had resolved otherwise, at home, I was still fixated on work. I'd study my scripts until I fell asleep only to find them in the middle of the night or the next morning, unmoved on my chest. I had not even budged in my sleep. As our wonderful Gena turned three, the time which I had spent enjoying and caring for her had been nil compared to the time I had spent on the phone, which rang, on average, every three minutes with work-related conversations. I was all the while assuring Janet that when *M*A*S*H* was over I would return to the quiet, contented "Birdman" she had originally fallen in love with and I would also be a better father. Part of me knew she wasn't buying it . . . and that part of me was beginning to panic.

I fully intended to keep my promise, but I was begging her to just hold on until my responsibilities on *M*A*S*H* had ended. Either film work or theater work would be lucrative but far less demanding on our time. With both, we could plan how many weeks a year I would work. An eleven-week shoot on a film would pay so well, I would not have to work again for a year. That would leave plenty of time to be a full-time dad and husband at home. The same was true, though less lucrative with theater.

But Janet didn't understand show business. I could see in her eyes she didn't believe me. I had lost her trust. And my uptight behavior was increasing as I pushed myself to achieve higher levels of excellence at work.

One afternoon at the studio I asked for a private meeting with Larry and Gene, in Gene's office. Private meetings were always granted apprehensively by them. They often meant their cast member might toss a "bombshell" — more money . . . better billing . . . complaints about fellow workers. What I wanted to request was a *Christian name for Radar*. From the time of the feature, I knew that any character tagged with a nickname would, if successful, become one-dimensional fodder for crossword puzzles in newspapers, jokes at private gatherings and the monologue on *The Tonight Show*. With Larry and his well of artful writers, we could humanize him. "What name would you like?" Larry asked.

It hadn't occurred to me to suggest one. "Walter," I heard myself respond.

When I left the office on the way back to the set, I considered my curious subconscious reason for choosing that name. I remembered Walter Pitkie, my gentle, good-hearted playmate from Forestville. I stopped on the walk and wept. He was the best and truest part of me. The part that I had oppressed and alienated in order to appear tough and powerful in a threatening world. Through my performances, however, I could express him; I could be who I wished to be again, who I truly was inside and, if I could dispense with the duality I retained from my dysfunctional family background, I could express him in my daily life as well. Gena would like "Walter" for a Daddy.

But, personality transformation is easier wished for than achieved. Worldly analysis and therapy had proven disappointingly unsuccessful. It falls into God's province. But, God had not been on my mind for many years. Though I didn't know it, I was about to be reborn. Within two weeks, a script would appear on our discussion table (which we proudly referred to as "the round table"). It would be titled "Quo Vadis, Captain Chandler," and the author was Burt Prelutsky. The plot line, concerning a soldier with a severe head wound being admitted to the 4077th Hospital, would prove prophetic. He claimed to be Jesus Christ. All the medics considered his case one of mental derangement; all but Radar. Radar's heart was open enough to accept the possibility. At the very end of the script would be a scene in which the patient was about to board the homeward bound bus. Radar appears with his teddy bear, the man looks at him and Radar says timidly, "I was wondering, sir, if you wouldn't mind . . . could you please bless my bear? I know he isn't real, but we're very close." The kind, wounded soldier, his head still in bandages, smiles and places his hand gently on Radar's teddy bear, and blesses it. Then he places his hand on Radar's forehead and says ". . . and bless you too, Radar." Radar's eyes well up in tears and he says, "My name is Walter."

Larry had overseen Prelutsky's script and added the ending. What a wonderful way to introduce Radar's real name.

A name. I had a real name also and it wasn't "Radar." We take a name for granted. Everyone has one. Everyone has always had one.

Why? What is so important about having a name? Why not just, person number 728A? Why is the name of whatever God we choose to believe in important?

On a charity fundraising trip to my Wisconsin hometown of Delavan, my high school principal told me a very odd thing. Do you remember that psychic who our school hired for that "paid assembly" to speak about ESP? He had peaked through the stage curtain just before he went on. The principal was standing next to him. "Who's the boy in the second row with the plaid long-sleeve shirt?" The clairvoyant asked. My principal had responded, "His name is Gary Burghoff, he's sixteen years old and a recent transplant from Connecticut." The psychic said, "Someday everyone will know him, but no one will know his name . . ."

His prophetic observation had come true!

Now, no matter where I traveled, people (even some family members) referred to me as RADAR. Though, I loved my character, each time they called me by that fictional name, it was as though they were stabbing my heart. Radar had stolen my identity and I was lonely. So too is God, I thought as I stood there on the walk. I once again resolved to learn his true identity.

By *M*A*S*H*'s seventh season, I had given the studio notice that when my seven year-contract had ended, I would be leaving. No one knew that my marriage was also ending. Janet had finally had enough. To me, the tragedy was that, once I left the show and we were able to catch our breath, she would realize that we were the same two people we were when we met — with the same values, hopes, and desires. But, we had already separated and she had found someone else. We agreed that Gena would remain with me, in the Malibu house, for two years. Though, she never shared her reason, I assumed it was to solidify her relationship with her new mate, while affording Gena a more stable transition by allowing her to remain with Dad in her familiar Malibu surroundings.

When Radar's final episode was finished, I became a single parent. Though devastated by our pending divorce, I was thankful for the opportunity to raise my daughter. She was the only sunshine left in my life.

She had a little playmate down the street named Bridget Anderson, who was also four years old. While buying them a burger at McDonald's one afternoon, I decided to test their imaginations with a little game. I took a French fry off my plate and placed it flat on the table.

"What's that?" I asked them.

"A French fry," they responded in unison.

Then, I tore elongated pieces from another fry to simulate branches on a tree trunk. "Now what is it?" I asked, in a more excited tone.

"A TREE!", they shouted gleefully.

I pinched and applied smaller pieces. "How 'bout now?"

"LEAVES!" they shouted.

With tinier bits, which I sprinkled below the "branches," I asked, "What's falling to the ground?"

"SEEDS! they screamed. "And when the seeds begin to sprout, what's going to grow?" I excitedly asked.

"FRENCH FRIES!" they both exclaimed.

Kids have a fabulous way of holding on to reality even in the midst of fantasizing.

On the beach one afternoon, Bridget ran up to me with a shell she had found. "Isn't that pretty?" I said.

In a minute, she ran up with another, more perfectly formed one. "Oh!" I exclaimed. "That one is even prettier!"

Once again she returned, this time with a deeply pitted dull, worn, misshapen remnant of a shell, which had been nearly obliterated by time and the elements. Trying to be "honest," I said, "That one's not as pretty as the others."

"I know," she responded; "this one's *BEAUTIFUL.*"

Upon second consideration, I saw the beauty. It was in its character. I also saw that the shell reminded me of me.

When I would tuck Gena into bed at night and the house became quiet and semi-dark, I would often go to my chair in the living room, sit and weep. One afternoon, when Gena was in Montessori school, the phone rang. It was my father's doctor in Connecticut, where he and my mom had retired.

"Gary, it's Dr. Brown."

"What's going on?"

"Hasn't . . . hasn't anyone called you yet?"

"No. What's the matter?"

"Oh . . . I . . . two days ago, an ambulance brought your dad into Essex Hospital. At first we thought he had a coronary and we put him in I.C.U., but later I . . . I thought he had pneumonia, so we . . . I took him out of intensive care."

"What's his condition?"

"Well . . . I was wrong . . . later that night he . . . he had a second heart attack and . . . *we lost him.*"

My legs gave out and I dropped to my knees.

"Are you all right?"

" . . . "

"I'm sorry . . . I thought your family would have called you by now."

I had plane tickets for Connecticut already purchased two days earlier. Part of the unfinished business I wanted to accomplish after leaving *M*A*S*H* was to get closer to my father. I was on my way home. But I was too late.

As I drove to school to pick up Gena, the news over the radio contained information of my father's death. If Dr. Brown hadn't phoned, I would have learned it driving along Pacific Coast Highway. In less than a week, my marriage was over, my career had ended and my father had died. I felt as if I would also die. I was now only living for Gena.

That night, after reading her a bedtime story, and waiting for her to fall asleep, I went to the living room, fell on my knees and prayed. *"Lord, whatever you think of me, I want you to know that I love you and appreciate all the underserved blessings you have given me. Dear God, I don't know how to do this but . . . I'm empty inside . . . nothing is right. I don't know what to do. Please. Enter my heart and fill me with your wisdom and knowledge. I give myself over completely to you."*

Gena and I took the red-eye flight the next night to Connecticut. We were to attend my father's funeral. When we returned a week later the miracles began — I began getting letters from fans who were writing that they were receiving "impressions" of me and offered prayers for my happiness. I picked up my Bible, opened it and to my amazement, though I had tried a thousand times, without comprehension, I began to understand every single word. Packages were suddenly being delivered, containing religious literature of every religion and denomination. One contained a book called *The Aquarian Gospel of Jesus the Christ,* and all were from total strangers.

One evening while showering, I tried to ease my sorrow by "scat singing" like Ella Fitzgerald, but amazingly, what came out were words in a foreign language! I was speaking in tongues! The words had no meaning to my ears or mind, but my heart understood and I felt uplifted and refreshed!

Friends, who previously only talked about the weather, were now sharing information about how God was working in their lives! And Jehovah's Witnesses were suddenly knocking on my door to Bible study with me. For the first time, I accepted. While driving, I began to "mis-read" billboard signs. One which advertised "Hal's Junction," I read as *HALLELUIAH!*

The sky suddenly became a fascination. At night I would spend hours marveling at the order of the Universe! I was realizing that planets only collide to form new planets and stars revealing a *continuing planned and orderly creation*!

And my attention once again fell to the natural world around me. Our world. Planet Earth.

No matter how hard our scientists tried, they found no other life among the billions of planets in the universe, but we were in no way alone! We were *unique* — created for a particular and wondrous reason paramount to God's plan!

Though "the age of miracles" had apparently passed, according to the world, I was becoming a living example that the world was dead wrong. I was a miracle! My crucifixion was being transformed into my rebirth! Crucifixion? The tabloid press was writing exaggerated stories of my on-the-set transgressions. Some within the public were jeering at me and rebuking my integrity on the street. I'd wanted to lend my services to charitable causes, but I felt my creditability would reflect badly on them. My life had completely disintegrated. But, *the blood from my bleeding side wound, which fame had inflicted, was becoming the death wound inflicted on Christ just before his RESURRECTION. My crucifixion stake was being transformed into JACOB'S LADDER. PRAISE GOD. PRAISE JEHOVAH THROUGH CHRIST!*

Finally, I knew his NAME.

≫ ≫ ⁂ ≪ ≫

In 1976, I had bought a waterfront cottage on a private pond in Connecticut. Gena and I now returned there for the summer. The cottage was rustic (to say the least). In places, you could see daylight through the single-wall construction. The three hundred acres of second growth forest around us and the wild living creatures which visited our yard provided serenity and beauty. Caring for Gena, still four years old, was a full days' proposition, albeit a joyful one. Each night, after she fell asleep around 8:00, I would continue working, cleaning and preparing an orderly house for the next day's adventure in single parenting. I wouldn't hit the sack until one or two in the morning. Gena was up at five a.m. She would enter my room and gently nudge my arm until I'd awaken. One morning, after five nights of sleep deprivation, I opened a reluctant eye and told her, "Oh, no sweetheart, daddy needs more sleep in the mornings. Otherwise, I can't be a good Daddy. You play with your toys in your room when you wake up each day, until Daddy gets up . . . okay?"

"Okay," she agreed, as she began to walk back to her room.

"Unless it's an emergency," I added.

She looked at me curiously, smiled and left.

The next morning at five a.m., I awakened to the usual persistent nudge from Gena's little hand. I parted my heavy eyelids to find her coyly leaning on my bedspread.

"Is a *bat in the toilet* an emergency?" she gently asked, fluttering her eyelids and grinning.

I ran into the bathroom to find a bat doing the "sidestrokes" in the commode!

We had other visitors. Raccoon families soon learned of our presence and our food. We'd awaken to find the screen to our porch torn open with forgotten groceries missing. Each night Gena and I would eagerly wait in semi-darkness to catch a glimpse of furry friends who also occupied our getaway cabin. I was in heaven again, as I had been in Harwington as a boy. And now, Gena was being given the same privilege the Lord had granted me. My heart was again being nurtured by His creation.

Along with the religious books, I hungered to read, I also kept an eye out for inspirational autobiographies and non-fiction worldly material. I was determined not to become a "Holy Roller" and was resolved to remain firmly grounded on earth while allowing my spiritual yearnings to soar. While browsing through the psychology section in a local bookstore, my eyes fell upon Dr. Herbert Freudenberger's bestselling book, *Burn Out*. That phrase was constantly bandied about in Hollywood. It was a cliché ("I'm getting burned out on sushi" would be a good example). I had learned that you could almost always judge a book by randomly opening it to any page. If that page held material which interested you, the book was worth buying. The page I arbitrarily selected, included, "Burn Out is a clinically diagnosed disorder, which is treatable and completely curable." As soon as I returned home, I was calling information.

"Operator? I'm looking for the number in New York of a Dr. Herbert Freudenberger."

"One moment. Yes . . . we are connecting you."

This seemed too easy.

As I was being connected, I glanced at the book's back cover biography. Freudenberger was the President of the National Association of Psychiatrists. This was an important guy I was about to speak with. How could he be this available? *Maybe the operator is connecting me to some other Dr. Herbert Fraudenberger.*

"Hello, this is Dr. Freudenberger," a kind voice proclaimed.

"Doctor . . . Are you the author of *Burn Out?*"

"Yes I am. To whom am I speaking?"

I was flabbergasted and a bit nervous.

"Doctor . . . You don't know me . . . well, in a way you might. I'm the actor who's been playing Radar on *M*A*S*H*."

"Yes, Mr. Burghoff. I'm a fan."

He actually knew my name.

"Doctor, I hope this isn't an imposition, but for over two years I've had these symptoms —."

"Stop right there," he interrupted. "Let me describe them for you. See if I'm correct."

As I listened, he described (in every last detail) what had befallen me at work and at home.

"You see, Gary, 'Burn Out' is a modern disorder, which affects the primarily ambitious and highly motivated among us; people who struggle all their lives, often from childhood, to reach a lofty goal. But when they, through dedication, hard work and sacrifice, finally *reach* that goal, it is usually not what was expected."

As with my first experience with that store window television, I stood there jaw-slackened and astounded. He was describing in one analytical paragraph, MY LIFE.

He continued: "When they are finally facing the reality of the work place, they experience denial instead of disappointment. Instead of recognizing the world, they have dreamed about for what it truly is — extremely imperfect — they struggle harder and harder to compensate, becoming PERFECTIONISTS, often feeling that the duality of the work experience is somehow their own fault. If I just try harder, they think, everything will be all right."

"But it isn't," I blurted.

"No. By this time they are caught in a vicious whirlpool. The more they strive, the more mentally distressed they become. The more distressed, the harder they strive! Then, the physical breakdown begins to occur and the irritability at work, and usually at home also. It becomes, in many cases, quite severe. But, as soon the 'victim' becomes savvy enough to leave the work situation, he begins almost immediately, to return to normal. In fact, he's often much more normal and wiser from the experience. This is entirely a work-oriented disorder."

"Do they become more spiritual or religious?" I asked.

"Not necessarily. They just return to who they were, only, as I said, often wiser and better able to move on."

I felt entirely that I had been speaking to a beautiful human being. His kind and gentle countenance and brilliant analysis renewed my confidence in modern psychiatry and *in humanity.*

But Burn Out had just ruined my marriage, my hope of reconciliation with my father and had driven me to disrupt and confuse my beloved *M*A*S*H* family as well. If my growing faith and spiritual knowledge had not entered my life, I would very likely have shown up on a coroner's lengthy list of "probable suicides." Regardless of the fact that I had the disorder, I was still responsible for my behavior. After praying, I shot a note off to Alan Alda.

Dear Alan,

I don't know if you or our cast mates can forgive me. I only want you to know that I regret deeply any pain I may have caused you. I never meant to hurt anyone.

Affectionately,
Gary

In a week I received his response.

Dear Gary,

I want you to know that I interpreted your letter with nothing but the warmth and sincerity you intended. It's the pressure of the work which caused our mutual irritabilities. You are still loved!

As Always,
Alan

There it was, BURN OUT.

Alan was also in the "whirlpool." By the eleventh year, he would announce his difficult but necessary decision to close the curtain on Stage Nine at Twentieth Century-Fox. I know he soon returned to his normal, wiser, and wonderful self.

ఌ ఌ ಅ ಳ ఌ

One autumn afternoon, while still at the pond cottage, I received a phone call . . .

"Hello, Gary?" spoke a vaguely familiar voice.

"Who's calling?"

"It's John Chapin. You remember me?"

I did — and warmly. He was my very respected and enjoyable sixth-grade teacher at Bingham School in Bristol.

"CHICK! (That was his affectionate nickname). My lord, it's been a lifetime. How are you?"

"I'm fine, thanks. I've been married to my wife, Bea, for a lot of years now and we've been very happy."

"To what do I owe the pleasure of your call?"

"Well, Bea and I heard that you had returned, and we were wondering if you'd give us the honor of witnessing to you . . ."

"You sound like a Jehovah's Witness!" I joked.

"I . . . I mean, we are." (He had been a Catholic when I had known him.)

"John, you are welcome in my home, anytime . . ."

Before they arrived, I had already slipped into my "non-joiner," rebellious, truth-seeking and dogma-resistant self. I was ready for a sparring match. But, especially opposite Bea, *I was no match at all!*

"Look around you. You see the beauty, the order? That's the system of God. Everything other than nature is the system of man and corrupted!"

I had no argument.

John spoke. "You see, in Genesis, we read Jehovah's master plan. He created this physical world with the intent of it becoming a paradise."

Still no argument.

"We are all descendants of the first man and woman," Bea continued. "We were created to love, enjoy, and care for God's paradise — Earth — and, to give joyful thanks to him for life and beauty!"

I sat passively without disagreement.— *Come on you two, give me something to argue about,* I thought.

"When the angels rebelled in heaven, Jehovah, who creates all with free will, needed a stage and actors to play out his triumphant victory before the undecided angels. He created us with free will to prove that we would eventually reject Satan and come back to HIM."

Sounded like a plausible concept. I liked the part about the stage and actors —.

"Jehovah is not just great, he is greater, has more power and intellect than we can possibly imagine!"

Sounded like God to me.

"His promise to us (and our hope is based on that promise) is that through Christ's forfeit on the stake, we will once again become the perfect souls He originally created, and we will live forever, without death on a *paradise* Earth. Any questions?"

Now I had one, a rebellious one.

"Yes, how do you know Jesus Christ wasn't just some guy who only thought he might be the Son of God? How do you know he wasn't just some nut?"

Bea's eyes lit like fire!

"LOOK!" she shouted. "I can answer that, but I'm not about to tell you what you should believe. *I'm telling you what I believe!*"

That is not only entirely fair, I thought. *It's refreshing. This woman is a holy spitfire!*

For the next three hours, they shared much of their considerable knowledge. They showed me how the Bible was an ingenious mosaic of social commentary and prophecy, which from its beginning through Jesus' birth, supported and foretold his arrival and mission. His mission was to pay the ransom for our sins, to purify us and make it possible for us to once again walk forever with Jehovah in "the Garden" (paradise Earth).

By the time they finished, I knew that if I was going to profess any religious discipline, what they had just shared, was it. They had respected me as they respected the Bible — by reason — not by blind faith.

For the next two years, *The New World Translation of the Holy Scriptures Bible*, which they had given me, never left my side. The wisdom it contained fascinated me. I would carry it to the store, into the bathroom, on planes, trains and in automobiles. I'd never preach to others, but I was always willing to witness the miracles Jehovah was working in my life. And here's one of them . . .

Toward the end of my first year with Gena, Janet phoned to insist that Gena be flown to her. She had resettled in a remote area of New Mexico and had made a home for her. I didn't want to give her up, but I felt it was cruel to deny her mother's wish. So instead of two years, I had only one; one very happy and special year. Janet and I then agreed that I would have liberal, but *unspecified* visitation rights.

Gena and I flew to the airport in New Mexico, where I transferred her into her mother's care and flew on to L.A. and Malibu, again. A month or two went by, and I missed her. Christmas was approaching and I called Janet to request that I visit Gena for a week over the holidays.

Now, there is something about divorce; it's a process. Although we had parted traumatically, with time we had resolved to forgive and move on. But, while we were separated and had time to be alone with our guilt, remorse and whatever else surfaces from the depths, one or both of us would inevitably experience anger. At this time, it was Janet's turn.

Her response to my request was, "I don't think it's a good idea. You won't like it here. These people don't like 'television people.' They're too real."

REAL? What was I, Some kind of Disney cartoon?

Now, I had studied the network ratings and I knew that even people in remote places such as New Mexico watch and enjoy *television*. I wasn't too worried about being tarred and feathered. But Janet's irrational, angry rhetoric gave me pause. *What kind of place had she moved to?* My active imagination ignited images of an Indian Village or mountain men and women in fringed doeskins on horseback carrying rifles with bear traps dangling from their saddles.

After pleading my rights as Gena's father, she reluctantly relented and tersely spit out some confusing directions to Ruidoso, New Mexico. These directions hadn't included her street address, leading me to wonder if there were any streets in Ruidoso. I still had images of teepees and totem poles. Bear in mind, I'd never been to New Mexico. It was a mystery, and a long drive from Southern California.

I left on a Wednesday; by Friday I made it to El Paso, Texas. I phoned Janet from a motel to double check the directions. I asked her to estimate my driving time from El Paso. She estimated "eight, maybe ten hours." She still omitted her street address. I left early the next morning, following the confusing directions, and arrived in Ruidoso an hour later than expected. As soon as I checked into a motel, I phoned Janet, who was *furious!*

"Your daughter waited up for you for hours! I finally put her to bed! Call *tomorrow* at 9 a.m. I'll decide then, when *and if* you can see her!" And she hung up again — without giving me her street address!

There were streets there, after all. There were also about a thousand very nice homes and a multitude of condominiums! Ruidoso was a thriving resort town, which, in season, catered to wealthy Texans and vacationers who attended horse races at Ruidoso Downs Racetrack. In the winter, it thrived as a ski resort. *Not a teepee in sight.*

Shaken by Janet's anger and the uncertainty over whether or not my eleven hundred-mile trip to be with Gena had been a good idea, depression was setting in. I was hungry. It was 9:15 p.m. I asked the man in the motel office where the nearest restaurant was.

"No restaurant open this time of night . . . you can try the bar across the street . . . maybe they'd make you a sandwich."

I wandered over to the bar and as I entered, the aroma of rawhide and beer swirled through my nostrils. I viewed several people at the bar and a few couples seated at tables. Now, I don't usually mind dining alone, but I was immediately drawn to a young couple seated off to one side. A curious feeling prompted me to do something I had never done. I asked if they'd mind if I joined them. They welcomed me warmly without recognizing me from *M*A*S*H*. They were also Born-Again Christians, who were eager to share their joy in the Lord.

Now, you may be saying "So what?" Up to this point, I might agree except for the feeling I had just experienced. It was unique. It was as if I knew I had to meet these exact people; as if I were being directed to meet them.

My mind soon dismissed the occurrence as we enjoyed conversation over sandwiches and coffee. Afterward, they asked if I cared to join them at their condo for dessert. We were sitting in their living room having desert when I became flushed with sudden indignation, stemming from my frustration over being so close to (and yet so far from) my little girl.

I excused myself and asked if I could use their phone. I was suddenly determined to call Janet and demand she divulge her street address, so that I would be assured of being at Gena's door without further delay in the morning.

Now *I* was angry.

The phone was next to a window. As Janet's phone was ringing in my ear, I saw a woman in the house directly across the street answer her phone. IT WAS JANET, not more than a hundred feet before me! Out of a gazillion condos and homes, the Lord had led me directly to Gena!

All my anger, frustration and apprehension disappeared and I was suddenly grateful and calm, as Janet answered, "Hello."

"Hi, it's me. I just phoned to say that I know your address and I'll see you first thing in the morning."

As I returned to my gloomy motel room, I felt the warm glow of angels around me. My depression had lifted and I slept easily, calmly and deeply all night long.

ั ั ଔ ั ั

To the masses who largely viewed television as the standard in evaluating an actor's success, I had fallen into a black hole in 1979. But, in a very true sense, my life was just beginning. As an actor, the Lord was providing some of my best opportunities. My primary training had been for the stage. *M*A*S*H* made it possible for me to draw theater audiences. I was deluged with offers from regional and dinner theaters nationwide to appear in productions such as *The Owl and the Pussycat* which Alan had originated on Broadway (pre-*M*A*S*H*); *Play it Again, Sam*, Woody Allen's charming fantasy comedy; *Whose Life Is It Anyway?*, Brian Clark's comedy-drama concerning a quadriplegic's right to pull the plug on his life; Larry Shue's *The Nerd*, a unique and original comedy in which I starred on Broadway; and an original play written with me in mind, called *A Good Look at Boney Kern*. I played the latter in more than eleven theaters, breaking house attendance records coast to coast for over five years!

My fortuitous role in Dick Clark's fantasy Christmas film *The Man in the Santa Claus Suit* allowed me to co-star with one of the true geniuses of Hollywood's Golden Age: Fred Astaire. In my first scene with him, I quickly learned what a kind and generous man he was. We were shooting on location on New York's Westside in a little jewelry shop. On a break, a production assistant approached Mr. Astaire to inform him that the press had gotten wind that he was working in town and had begun to spontaneously congregate outside the shop on the street. They were requesting an impromptu sidewalk interview. Mr. Astaire agreed under the condition that his co-star (me) would share the limelight with him. Remember, this was the *New York* press. It was the *Daily News*, the *Post* and the *New York Times*. A photo with a star of his magnitude would be syndicated worldwide, and he knew it.

We casually walked out of the shop, onto the sidewalk together. And, as the photographers began snapping their lenses, Fred Astaire leaned against me, a casual and graceful elbow on my shoulder, in a physical attitude which suggested that I was a member of his family. I can never forget that kindness. Nor can I forget the film. It has played on National Television *every year* since 1979, as a Christmas classic.

Later that year my divorce from Janet became finalized. Our Malibu house was for sale and we had cashed in our other real estate chips, dividing the net profits by half as a settlement. Janet generously quitclaim deeded the Connecticut cottage to me and I paid her a small amount in lieu of alimony, in addition to half of my future *M*A*S*H* residuals. Neither of us had any idea, at the time, that they would still be rolling in twenty-seven years later!

The real estate boom of the 1970s had collapsed and I lived in the Malibu house until 1981, waiting for a buyer. One morning in the spring of that year, I dressed in natural leather clothing, a red sash around my waist and joined my best friends, Frank and Theresa Anderson, (Bridget's Mom and Dad) at the Los Angeles Renaissance Fair, being held in the Santa Monica Mountains.

Though two years had passed since my divorce, I was still pining. I had dated and "fooled around," but my new Christian conscience was gradually dissolving old worldly habits and desires. Spiritual rebirth for me was a process, not an immediate, immaculate, magical transformation. Cynical non-believers often confused "spiritual growing pains" with hypocrisy. A new Christian has taken a new, much narrower road, but he still has a long way to travel before he cleanses himself of a lifetime of worldly habits. Though guided forward, backsliding is frequent. But the Holy Spirit convicts you each time you transgress and, little by little, "pleasure" begins to become far less important. It is eventually transformed into joy.

Among the valuable lessons I had learned from the Witnesses were new definitions of the words "guilt" and "conscience." Conscience is imprinted in us by Jehovah. It is an integral part of being created "in His image." Guilt, on the other hand, is the crushing tool, used by Satan, which leads to depression and hopelessness. The Holy Spirit convicts lovingly and persistently through conscience and eventually uplifts us!

The fair was alive with medieval activity. Archers, duelers and minstrels roamed the dirt roads as the merchants' booths, adorned with hand-fashioned period jewelry, leather goods and candied fruit, amused us. Suddenly, I caught a glimpse of a stunning blonde in a flowing white-lace dress. As she walked before me on the way to her booth, I heard myself say to Frank, "I'm going to marry that woman." He chuckled as if I was kidding, but soon realized I was dead serious.

"Just like that," he mused. "Don't you think you should meet her first?"

Sounded like a reasonable idea . . .

I placed the pheasant-feathered mask I had just purchased over my face to avoid her recognizing my celebrity, and approached her. Feigning interest in whatever it was she was selling (Renaissance auto insurance for all I knew), I rattled off a few one-liners and stuttered a couple of sincere compliments regarding her beauty. She asked where I lived. I said, "Right here in Malibu, but I'm about to leave town for a few months to do theater . . . I mean . . . on business."

"I'm looking for a house in Malibu to rent," she said. "Would you be interested in renting me yours while you're away?"

I had no such interest, but if it would mean seeing her again, I'd consider it. We exchanged phone numbers.

The phone rang the next afternoon.

"Hi, it's Elisabeth, remember me?" (I had thought of nothing or no one else since the previous day.) "I was wondering if I could stop by and see the house . . . I'm minutes away."

As soon as I hung up the phone, I shed my garden-soiled sweatshirt and blue jeans and put on a casual sweater and slacks. She was about to find out I was a "famous actor" and I wanted to appear modestly cavalier and cool.

As her car drove into the driveway, I tripped on the hall carpet, knocking over a potted plant which distributed wet, potting soil all over my sweater. When the doorbell rang, I was back in the bedroom, frantically trying to change into a fresh shirt! I approached the door with my buttons misaligned and my fly partially opened! I "adjusted" myself frantically, as she waited at the doorstep. As I zipped up, she smiled at me through the front-door window! I had a hundredth of a second to appear cool again before opening the door and there was still some damp, gritty potting soil in my right shoe! I don't think I made it. Trying to act "natural" (but failing miserably), I let her in.

She was wearing a white linen summer dress, with flowered appliqués across her bodice. Her clear blue eyes and warm smile made me forget about my right shoe and its irritating contents. As I greeted her and guided her through the house, I glided along on marshmallows.

We joked and laughed and by the time we had returned to the living room, I kissed her.

"Gary," she whispered. "I like you, but *I'm not going to sleep with you.*"

Okay, I thought *I can live with "like."*

By the time she left an hour or so later, we had agreed that she would "housesit" while I was away in San Antonio, Texas.

⁓ ⁓ ଔ ⁓ ⁓

A Good Look at Boney Kern, by Chicago-based playwright author Jonathan Daily, is a tender little comedy-drama about a mid-western English teacher, who after a shockingly embarrassing love-affair in his youth, had chosen a life of celibacy.

He responds to a "ROOM FOR RENT" sign in an old Victorian house inhabited by a cantankerous, man-hating old woman and her gentle blind granddaughter, Julie. During the course of the play, though resistant to commitment, Boney falls in love with Julie. To his dismay and shock, in the second act, he is coerced by the grandmother (who has learned she is dying) into "impregnating" her granddaughter so that she will not be alone in the world. In the end, grandma dies and Boney stays with Julie, who is carrying their child.

It may not sound like much in synopsis form, but once produced, we realized we had a refreshing new hit on our hands. The audiences and the critics loved it! It was "only dinner theater" but the play was not usual dinner-theater fare. It was funny, tender and sensitive, and it touched people who saw it and came back a second time to see it again, deeply. Evidently, sexual insecurity and fear of commitment were universal and no other author had tapped into the subject.

Each evening after rehearsal, I would rush back to the condo (which the theater had provided) to write Elisabeth a letter. This went on daily for a month. She would respond in kind, and little by little, we were falling in love by mail. At the beginning of the second month of my run, I phoned her to ask if she would join me in San Antonio for a visit. It was a visit which would last eleven years.

We lived together for four years, as we traveled from theater to theater throughout America together. She helped to plan my busy schedule and her bright and gregarious social skills and energy helped to ease my fear of going out in public. The Lord was preparing me for resurrection, but Elisabeth was bringing me back to life. *We glowed together.*

Between theater bookings, we returned to the Connecticut cottage, which was undergoing a complete remodeling in preparation of our marriage. My visitation rights having been solidified by the courts: Gena would be flown from New Mexico for all holidays and summer vacations. She and Elisabeth hit it off immediately, and Elisabeth became a good surrogate mother.

But there was a fatal flaw in our relationship, which, in my love for her, I was overlooking. I was *"working to live."* My nearly fatal experience with Burn Out had taught me a valuable lesson about myself and I was not about to let it happen again. To Elisabeth, a husband *"lives to work."* I would learn that nothing I achieved or built for her was ever enough.

She began to complain that the cottage didn't feel like "home" to her. She wanted a real house. To me, the cottage symbolized a life of simplicity that I passionately sought after having "gone Hollywood." We were frequently at the famous Showboat Theater in Clearwater, Florida. We had bought a cozy two-bedroom waterfront condo in St. Petersburg. I was no stranger to St. Pete. I had gone through the first grade there as a child, living with my grandparents for the winter, while my parents were in Europe on matters concerning my Dad's business. I loved Florida and visited them growing up, nearly every winter over Christmas vacations. Elisabeth enjoyed it too, and was satisfied to make it our winter home.

But the Condo Association did not allow children and Elisabeth was pregnant. When our baby was born, we would have to move. I was very happy to return to Connecticut, but made the same fatal mistake my dad had made. I relented to Elisabeth's persistence over building a bigger and better "real" house and we purchased two acres on the water in Marathon, in the Florida Keys. Like my father before me, my desire to "keep peace" in my marriage resulted in building a house beyond my means and set us on a path to financial disaster.

ڝ ڝ ℭ ڝ ڝ

By this time in my career, I had dispensed with agents. In 1976, I met my manager, Bob Crystal. He was a loyal and good friend, whose background included production in the music recording industry and eventually, an association with Doris Day in her heyday, as her personal script reader. He had also managed Dean Martin's kids in a nightclub revue they had created and taken on world tour. Reg Grundy, the successful Australian film producer, had snagged Bob while touring the act "down under," and when I met him, he was independently employed at Grundy's L.A. production company. His financial independence and connection with the film industry made him a perfect choice as my representative. Though he could not, by law, negotiate my contracts, he served in an advisory capacity behind the scenes, while I negotiated my own job offers. I, being his only client, and he, being independently employed, gave him an edge which agents with a hundred competing clients could not offer. As soon as Bob came on the scene in my career, my *M*A*S*H* salary had doubled.

In 1985, just when the Lord knew I had thrust Elisabeth and myself into financial quicksand, Bob received a call from British Petroleum, the international Mega-oil Corporation. They were offering a high, six-figure contract for my services as spokesperson in their newly planned TV commercial campaign. I did some research and finding that BP was the most environmentally responsible of all the oil companies, we accepted the offer. For the next five years, our income from BP would underwrite my desire to be a stay-at-home dad and husband, and support the building of our Marathon home. I began to curtail my theater work.

My son, Miles Gustaf Rodney Burghoff, was born at Tampa Hospital, on June 19, 1986. We began construction on the Marathon property three months later. The property included water frontage on a deep-water canal complete with a two-story houseboat. The canal connected us with the clear blue waters of both the Atlantic and the Gulf of Mexico. It was a Caribbean paradise. When the house was finished, we had gone over budget by $120,000. The mortgage had become huge, yet my pride in the place and knowing that I had provided Elisabeth with her "heart's desire" was substantial.

A few weeks after we had moved in, Elisabeth's mother flew in from California for a visit. As soon as she walked through our door and viewed our three-bedroom, two-bath, ocean-view home, she giggled and said, "If my important developer friends in California saw this place, they'd laugh!"

I wasn't laughing. Now I knew where Elisabeth had been coming from. I was beginning to feel *trapped* in my marriage. The experience was all too reminiscent of my own mother's rejection of my first Christmas present.

But, as the years passed, our adorable Miles became a total joy and inspiration. From the time he was able to walk, he was *fishing!* I had never seen a boy take to the sport as did Miles. At five years old, he took his little Mickey Mouse, three-foot rod, with plastic spinning reel and hooked, played and landed an eighty-pound nurse shark, from the canal! I'd take him out to sea with me to troll for Dolphin fish and King Mackerel. On one occasion, he landed a twenty-pound Wahoo (one of the fastest and toughest game fish in the sea!) Our twenty-one foot, *Sea Sprite* fishing cruiser, would return daily with fresh fish for the dinner table. I loved him with all my heart. *Annulment was out of the question.*

Elisabeth, in addition to working as a dental assistant, had studied bookkeeping in college, she insisted on handling our financial matters. By the third year of my BP contract, she informed me that in order to continue our life style, I would have to earn $175,000 more a year. Though concerned, and definitely feeling pressured, I held on believing that the worst thing which could befall us would be the forced sale of the house. We could then reinvest in a more modest home. The real estate market in the Keys was brisk at the time.

My BP commercials were airing country wide (though never seen in New York, Chicago or L.A.) and the ample salary checks were flowing in monthly. Yet, I sensed we needed to plan for the worst.

One day while trolling offshore in the Atlantic, I viewed a large mass of floating rope which no doubt had been discarded from a ship at sea. As I trolled passed it, I noticed that it had become a floating ecosystem. Every level of the aquatic food chain was present in microcosm, from plankton, bait fish, to huge game fish. That little floating mass was a world of its own. My four trolling lines all engaged simultaneously! The result: four fine dolphin fish! Any floating mass, in these waters, was referred to by experienced fisherman as "a dolphin house." I analyzed the phenomenon. What were the principles involved? I concluded that baitfish, present in virtually all saltwater ecosystems, are attracted to food and shelter. They had an instinct that their reflective surfaces would attract predator fish (game fish). So, they would seek out not only food but shade, which would keep sunshine from causing reflection off their scales. If I could somehow control this principle with a device which would simulate favorable bait-fish conditions, a fisherman could use it to attract bait fish close to his boat thereby also attracting the game fish, which are ever seeking them. Some sort of floating device, which provided *food and shelter* around which baitfish would congregate, would also be a magical, highly effective *GAME FISH ATTRACTOR.*

For months, I would leave the house, and enter my backyard work shed. I had fashioned a miniature working model of the device I had imagined. It would be a floating platform, similar in form, to a small surfboard, about three feet long. In its center, it would hold a basket which, when filled with chum (frozen chopped fish parts) would distribute the defrosting particles from beneath its surface. The shape and size of the board would also provide shade and shelter, so the baitfish would feel safe and be reluctant to leave, even after the chum had been completely dispensed. It would be lowered by a line into the current, behind a drifting or anchored boat and fed out to the desired distance, off the stern, and then tied off. If it worked as planned, it could increase a fisherman's chances of a record catch by, I estimated, at least, two hundred percent!

Now, I had to build and test the thing.

I began frequenting the local hardware stores for available materials. It had to be made of strong yet buoyant parts. It also had to be constructed economically and designed efficiently for eventual manufacture. I settled on oiled Masonite for the surface material. It was waterproof, lightweight and tough enough to resist the elements. I would sandwich ordinary closed-cell insulation foam in between two matching Masonite boat-shaped forms. *Who would cut it?* I solicited help from a local cabinetmaker. I brought him a paper template I had cut to the preferred size and shape. Once he had completed the top and bottom Masonite plates, we sandwiched in the foam and drilled holes at the bow and stern inserting bolts to hold it together. Then with a band saw, we cut a rectangular hole in the center to accommodate a plastic basket I had selected. After insertion of the basket, a bungee cord would hold the basket's lid in place. A clip was added to the bow from which I could attach a line and I had *my prototype*!

I bought some chum at the bait store and headed out to sea in my boat. I anchored over the reef, just off Marathon, at a location where I had fished many times. Placing the chum in the basket and fastening the top, I lowered the device into the water and began feeding it back into the current. It drifted straight as I had hoped, and when I tied off the line, as it reached 40 feet, it straightened out and floated in the current as stable as my own boat at anchor. Now . . . *would it attract fish?*

I waited ten minutes, just watching for activity around the board. In fifteen minutes, I became impatient and I went to the bow and stood on the deck with a pair of binoculars I had brought.

As I focused, and the board came into clear view, *it was completely surrounded with every sort of baitfish! And they were not nervous baitfish! They felt perfectly safe as they schooled parallel to the board!*

Suddenly, the water began to boil violently! A school of King Mackerel attracted by the baitfish had rushed in to gorge themselves! But when they disappeared, instead of the remaining bait fish having fled, they had returned to the *safety of the board*! I had done it! Now, a fisherman had a target to cast to. No more hopeless guess work in an immense ocean. Now, the fish would come to the fisherman as if by magic! I called my device "chum magic" and proceeded immediately to build several prototypes. I had a local professional artist draw a logo, which pictured the board surrounded by leaping game fish. I had the rendering transferred to large, bright orange, oval-shaped stickers, which I applied to the bow surface of each of the five prototypes. *Next, I needed to test its attractiveness before the public.*

I had accepted an invitation to participate in the celebrity "Red Bone" Charity fishing tournament in Islamorada, a neighboring Key about sixty miles north of us. I called the hotel there, where a room had been reserved for me. I rented another room in which I would set up an attractive display featuring my invention. I prepared literature explaining the board's concept and function, which I planned (if I could get anyone to show up), to personally hand out.

Elisabeth and I checked into the hotel early on a Friday night. We asked the desk, if they would deliver our exhibit invitations to all the celebrity fishermen and women who were entered in the tournament. I'd hoped my *M*A*S*H* celebrity would pique their curiosity and they would flock to our presentation. They didn't. *Only one person showed up. The one the Lord had sent.* He was the sports columnist for the *Miami Herald* newspaper, the largest paper in the state. As I explained the principle of the board to him, his eyes lit up. I handed him a newly printed "Chum Magic" business card and he left. I fished the tournament and we went home.

Now, I had installed a new business phone a few days earlier in anticipation of *eventually marketing* "Chum Magic" once I had found a manufacturer to make it for me. Manufacturing and marketing, was the hard part. It would require months of negotiating for the best pricing on molds and materials. What I had shown my single visitor, at the hotel, was a *handcrafted prototype.* I was nowhere near ready to mass-produce the damn thing.

At 8 a.m. the next morning, that new business phone began to ring . . . and ring . . . *and ring.*

"Hello. I'd like to order that "Chum Magic" doohickey. The paper didn't say how much it cost. It doesn't matter. Can you ship it immediately? It's for a Christmas present."

The orders were pouring in on average of every four minutes! At 6 p.m. it would stop as if someone unhooked the phone. Then like clockwork, it would begin again at 8 a.m. Elisabeth ran out to buy a *Miami Herald.* That man had written a full-page article in the sports section, praising the new product, which promised to revolutionize the sport of salt-water fishing! The TV was arbitrarily tuned to CNN in the living room. As we were frantically writing down orders for the "phenomenal new product," which didn't even exist yet, we heard,

"And this just in . . . Guess who has just invented the greatest fishing tackle product since the fishhook? RADAR! — Joe Schmoe has the story . . ."

Our private phone rang.

"Gary, it's Mel. Are you watching CBS?"

"CBS? No, we're on CNN!"

"Flip the Channel. You're on CBS, news in the morning, too!"

Over the next two months, in order to fulfill our orders, we would have to *hand make every single* "Chum Magic" board and I hadn't even figured out the cost of making them! When the first call came in, I arbitrarily suggested a price of $49.95. By the time we, over the next few weeks, had taken ONE THOUSAND ORDERS, that's the price we were stuck with.

In two days, with the help of some friends, we converted our old houseboat into a full production line factory. The cabinetmaker, who leisurely had cut the original prototype, was suddenly and feverishly cutting, drilling and packing fifty boards a day. We were buying all the hardware retail, because we didn't have time to track down wholesale suppliers. The hardware store ran out of foam almost immediately and we were racing to Miami to gather truck loads.

And the phone *kept ringing*!

Newspapers all over the world had picked up the story and we were receiving orders from as far away as Spain.

We needed plastic bags of the correct size in which to wrap it and boxes needed to be special ordered in which to ship it. Yet, believe it or not, from November 2nd to December 19th of 1990 we *hand manufactured, wrapped and shipped one thousand and fourteen handmade "Chum Magic" boards in time for Christmas!* And we lost fifty cents on each and every one of them.

Then, we rested for two days and began researching plastics companies in Miami to help us manufacture the product that I had originally intended.

Before the end of December, I had rented a local commercial space to assemble the "Chum Magic" components supplied by the plastics companies. I hung a sign out front, which declared
"CHUM MAGIC"
PROUDLY MADE IN THE FLORIDA KEYS,
U.S.A.
By the time our real product hit the market, we were distributing to mom and pop fishing tackle and bait shops from Key West to California.

And then . . . the Gulf War hit, and all our orders *stopped.*

Though the product was selling well (now at $89.95), the humble retailers were so rattled by the mild recession and the sudden war that they stopped ordering anything that would retail for over twenty dollars. And that's a fact. Without orders or big bucks, Chum Magic Corporation was dead in the water before we had even learned to sail. While my new business was on the verge of bankruptcy, I (in desperation) managed to design a curved-butt-spinning rod. It was unique and provided the big game fisherman with much more fighting leverage combined with the convenience of spin casting.

The news reported that President and Mrs. Bush were vacationing on Islamorada. Now, George Herbert Walker Bush is an ardent fisherman. It seemed natural for me to select one of our finest rods, have someone prepare a nice wooden presentation case for it and present it unceremoniously to the President as a gift from me and Chum Magic Corporation. I didn't want it to seem that we were in anyway using him for publicity, so I simply drove it to Islamorada, where we located the President's staff (all very nice people) and, almost apologetically for the intrusion on their time, left the rod along with a business card. And then I went home. But the President's staff, it seemed, were fans and they recognized me.

The next morning at about 6 a.m. — while my slumbering subconscious mind was reaching desperately into the void trying to remember that dream I used to have as a child — I was torn away from slumberland by the persistent ringing of the telephone.

"Hell — . . . ah . . . Hello?"

"Mr. Burghoff?"

"I — I think so . . ."

"This is Major (?)."

"Excuse me?"

"I'm the President's aide, Mr. Burghoff."

"The . . . *President?*"

"Yes, sir — of the United States."

I sat upright in bed so fast it caused the air to vibrate in the room! (Two weeks later, a butterfly crashed in Indonesia!)

Elisabeth was now awake.

"Wha — what's the matter?" She stammered.

"Mr. Burghoff, are you —?"

"Yes, yes, I'm here! Is the President alright?"

He laughed.

"Yes, sir, the President's fine. I'm calling to extend his invitation to breakfast."

"Breakfast?" I looked at the clock; it was 6:04 a.m.

"Well, of course. Uh . . . *when?"*

"At *seven,"* he answered.

The road to Islamorada was a narrow, sometimes four-lane, mostly two-lane, thirty- to fifty-mile an hour, if there was light traffic (not likely when the President and the Secret Service were in town) NIGHTMARE! I had five minutes to jump out of bed, pull everything out of my closet and onto the floor until I found a decent dress jacket and slacks, not to mention matching shoes and clean shirt. Then I had to run to my $800 Renault and hope it would start, while gargling with my usual hydrogen peroxide and then, drive at thirty miles an hour *over* the top speed limit, in order to calmly and casually join the President and First Lady for breakfast. If you dissect that last word it's BREAK FAST!

Regrettably, Elisabeth couldn't come. The President had only invited me, and who would watch the boys? My little French import burned rubber as it left my driveway and wheezed and strained until it hit fourth gear. By that time, I was up to forty-five miles an hour! With pedal to metal for two-and-a-half anguishing minutes, it finally topped out at eighty and that's where it stayed for fifty-eight miles until I reached Islamorada. Almost immediately, however, just outside the Marathon town limits, a highway patrolman fell in behind me! I was sure he would pull me over. He remained so close to my rear bumper, at eighty miles an hour, if I had sneezed and let up one, one-thousandth of an inch on the throttle, I'd have been road kill! But, he didn't stop me! We just kept speeding together, the whole fifty-eight miles!

As we approached our destination, the road ahead was alive with military personnel, reporters and general onlookers. I spotted an empty spot on the side of the road and came to a screeching, dust-producing stop! I jumped out of the car as the highway patrolman was leaping from his.

"Why didn't you stop me?" I yelled.

"BECAUSE I'M LATE, TOO!" he shouted back, with a big grin on his face.

"Mr. Burghoff! Over here, sir!" a voice called.

I turned to see a handsome man in an immaculate military uniform, waving me on toward him. We shook hands as he asked, "Any trouble finding us?"

"No," I said, as I pulled up my sagging slacks and buttoned my wrinkled jacket (I think I also glanced down to check my fly).

"Please follow me, sir. The President and the First Lady are waiting."

I followed him up the stairs to the top level of a condominium complex and he opened the door for me. "Enjoy yourself, sir," he said as I entered.

To my right (on matching upholstered chairs behind a large coffee table) sat the President and Mrs. Bush. The President stood and offered his hand: "Well, Mr. Burghoff! So glad ya' could join us. I don't know how to thank ya' for that beautiful fishing rod!" After shaking his hand, I offered mine to the First Lady.

"Hello, Mrs. Bush. Are you enjoying the Keys?"

"Yes, I am. And *don't* ask me about wading!" she smiled.

It had been all over the news that she had gotten out of the President's boat while they had been Red fishing on the shallow flats a few days earlier. The persistent press had shot photos of her holding her skirt above her knees.

"It hadn't crossed my mind to do so," I smiled back.

I was offered one of the two chairs across the coffee table from them and, as someone served us coffee, we chatted about the weather, fishing conditions, yesterday's catch, and God only remembers what. I was so rattled from my eighty-mile-an-hour adventure in my flying French fry and finding myself suddenly and ostensibly chatting with the President of the United States, I could barely remember that my name was Jerry Berjof. But, I tried to appear "intelligent."

Suddenly, I became aware that there was another person in the chair next to me. To this day, I don't know who he was. But as he spoke, he seemed important.

"So, that rod you designed — can it catch Blue Fish?" he asked in a sarcastic tone.

"Well, it's designed for any big game fish from Black Fin Tuna to Marlin," I responded. "So it will surely handle a big Blue Fish."

"Good," he said. "George has trouble keeping them on his line off Kennebunkport."

The President didn't seem to find the comment particularly humorous, I felt, and he changed the subject: "So, what do ya' think about the result of the war?"

My God. He's asking ME about war? (We had just whipped Sadam Hussein's butt in Desert Storm.)

"Well, I think the new weapons, which we saw on TV were . . . I mean . . . the surgical nature of them . . . you know . . . only singling out military targets . . . and . . . fewer civilians being killed . . . I mean, you know . . . good."

I was in way over my head.

"I feel a new spirit in the country," he responded proudly. "Don't you?"

I had no idea how to answer him. The only "new spirit" I had felt watching the whole sad Gulf War unfold was the spirit of fear for my children's future in a dangerous world.

This was not an elitist who sat before me. He seemed like a very warm and genuinely concerned man. The mystery man to my left seemed to possess a slightly darker countenance. (Perhaps *he* was really the President in clever CIA/Hollywood makeup and the one across the coffee table was just a look-a-like impostor hired to keep me off guard while the *real* President to my left sized me up through fake, latex eyelids, I found myself thinking.)

Forcing my mind back to what appeared to be reality, I answered "I hope so, sir."

"Well then," said the President of the United States. "How's your new fishing tackle business going?"

Now, I had a bigger problem! George Bush was certain there was no recession. He had said so a dozen times at press conferences. I knew there *was*. My company was about to go under because of it. How the hell could I answer him? I opted for simple honesty.

"We were doing fine," I said. "But the recession is causing us some problems at the moment."

The room fell silent (perhaps only for a millisecond), but it seemed much longer. After a bewildering pause, he smiled and glanced at his watch. I knew this was a technique, started by Richard Nixon, twenty years earlier to indicate that *the meeting had ended.*

"Well, how about a photograph as a little remembrance of our all-too-short visit," he said. He stood, I stood. The mystery man stood and left the room. The First Lady remained seated, and a photographer came flying through a bedroom (it may have been a closet) door as the President of the United States led me before his lens.

Now we were standing very close! Having photos taken with fans of *M*A*S*H* was commonplace for me. I always placed my arm around them, so as to appear warm and fuzzy in the photograph when they showed it to their grandkids. So by habit, *I was putting my arm around the President of the United States!* George Bush is six-four; I'm five-five. If my arm had completed its intended motion, *my right hand would be resting on his hip!* I quickly withdrew my hand and, hoping Mrs. Bush had not noticed my momentary indecisiveness, I intuitively placed both hands in my pants pockets . . . *in my pockets? . . . in a photo with the President of the United States?* As I was in the embarrassing moment of pulling them out again, the photographer snapped the picture. I was then politely ushered out and I drove, in a daze, the legal speed limit home.

A week later, the President sent me the developed photo. I looked like Charles Laughton's Quasimodo! But he also included a kind note, which read. . . .

April 9, 1991

Dear Gary,

Here's a souvenir shot of our all-too-short visit at
Tarpon Flats last week. Thanks for coming all that
way. And, my special thanks for that beautiful fishing
rod. I will treasure it always.

Good Luck in your new business.
Sincere Best Wishes
George Bush

About the time President Bush was realizing he would lose the
next election, I was closing the doors to the Chum Magic Corporation
and my hope to save my family from bankruptcy.

ভ   ভ   ৫   ৠ   ভ

One afternoon while trolling alone, miles off shore in the sunny
Atlantic, I was amazed to have an avian visitor land on the stern of
my boat. My knowledge of sea birds was considerable due to my
Birdman of Malibu hands-on experience, twenty years earlier. But
this gull was unique. Its petite frame, gentle nature, and its "knowing
awareness" of me, as I looked back from my steering wheel (and its
unrecognizable physical markings, texture and solid beige color)
mystified me. It remained on my stern for several minutes, just
looking at me, and finally flew into the clear blue afternoon sky.

When I returned back to port, at our backyard dock, I was met
by a neighbor, who had been awaiting my return. I knew by her
concerned expression, something serious had happen. As I moored
my boat, she said, "Gary, I'm so sorry to have to tell you . . .
Elisabeth just called me by cell phone. She was speaking with your
Mom, up in Connecticut. She was taken to the hospital with an
irregular heartbeat early this morning. And, as she and Elisabeth
were speaking, she began coughing and she dropped the phone. A
doctor who was with her picked it up and informed Elisabeth she
had died."

It was October 31, 1991. That mysterious bird, which had visited
my boat, had done so at the exact moment of my mother's death. I

will not relive my very deep feelings here concerning my "crazy" mother's passing, but, if you will allow me, I include the following eulogy, which I wrote and delivered at her funeral.

EULOGY
ANN RICH BURGHOFF
1912–1991

There was a time in my youth, during those confusing teenage years, when because of being grounded for sagging grades or some other indiscretion, I was sure my mother was my worst enemy. Teenagers make many mistakes in their perceptions.

Now, at forty-eight years of age, from the vantage point of experience, I realize that she was then, continued to be with unwavering loyalty, and will forever be in my mind and my heart, my best friend.

When I left home at nineteen years of age to face a tough world, I soon learned to be tough myself in order to survive. But, there is a great difference between being tough as rubber in the sense of being resilient, flexible and tolerant and being cold and hard like steel in the sense of being insensitive to others. My mother always helped me to clarify the difference.

If I were to examine my phone bills for the last thirty years, my mother's number would be, by far, the most frequently apparent. I could call her to discuss virtually any feeling, any achievement or failure and she, more than any one individual, would listen and understand. I could tell her anything and know she felt what I felt, shared the burden of my losses and the joy of my success. And while my success was relished with pride, she, somehow, always reminded me that gentleness, charity and generosity were of even greater importance. My mother was the most generous person I have ever known. For her children, my brother David and I, there was no sacrifice too great. You could expect this from a mother, but it was extended to others as well, for both David and I to witness growing up.

One of my earliest recollections, as a very small child, was of a "panhandler" (today referred to as a "homeless person") knocking at our door on East Main Street in Forestville. In those post-war days, many were down and out and many were turned away. Not at our house, however. Not from our mother.

One look at the man's tattered shoes and Mother, without even closing the door on the man, with total trust of this stranger on our doorstep, disappeared upstairs and in a few minutes returned with, what appeared to be, every pair of shoes from my father's closet. You can imagine my dad's surprise when he returned from work to learn that the only pair of shoes he now possessed were those he was wearing. And, while I seem to remember a momentary annoyance on his part, I knew intuitively that he loved her for it.

Nearly thirty years later, just months before his own passing, he expressed his feeling for her, so passionately and strongly to me that each word is forever imprinted, verbatim, on my memory. He said, "Your mother is a damned unusual woman and I have loved her with all my heart from the first moment I laid eyes on her."

I only wish that with a little "Back-to-the-Future" magic, I could have been there for that first meeting. It is not too farfetched to picture Louis Rodney

Burghoff throwing a football at Rockwell Park when he spotted Ann Rich dancing her heart out with the children on the grass. There are those who still speak fondly of her charm and the incredible inner spirit her dancing expressed, for it was more than a form of entertainment to her. Her dancing expressed her very special celebration of life.

She was good — she was very, very good — and she could have been one of the great ones. But, she chose to dance with only one man and the children they would have together.

Life with my mother *was a dance*. You had to be on your toes to keep up with her. There was a time when she seemed to be involved with everything.

She taught us the importance of community involvement. She taught us to judge others by the content of their character and not their political or religious beliefs or the color of their skin. And, even when she was unsure of herself, she strove to instill confidence in her sons so that, even when she felt weak, we could learn to be strong.

She taught us honesty.

One day when I was six, I lifted a plum from a local sidewalk produce stand on my way home from school. After returning home, and she realized what I had done, she grasped me firmly (*very firmly*) by the arm and briskly walked me back to the store to apologize to the owner. It remains the longest quarter mile I've ever traveled and my greatest lesson in humility.

In those days, when we all left home, we usually, if not always, left our doors unlocked. That was because our neighborhood was occupied by people, such as my mom and dad.

My son, Miles, who is five years old, upon hearing that his Grandma had just "passed on to heaven," asked his mother if he could send her a present. Elisabeth asked him what he had in mind. He went to his room and returned with a beautiful helium-filled balloon he had been given at a party. They took it outside and released it into the air and watched it as it rose into the clear blue afternoon sky until it disappeared from sight.

To Miles, I say, Grandma loves your present very, very much. And so does your grandpa, who also went to heaven on the very same thirty-first day of October, twelve years ago. They love your present so much that they are celebrating by dancing in each other's arms in the most beautiful park there is . . . on the greenest grass anywhere.

Goodbye, best friend — See you soon — I'm glad you were my mother.

"Lord, why hast though forsaken me?" asked the weak drowning man, as he was about to sink in the vast desolate ocean, which surrounded him.

I sent you two rescue helicopters and a Coast Guard cruiser," was the Lord's response.

"I know," gulped the poor drowning soul. "But, I've been waiting for you to save me, Lord!"

"You've already been saved," answered God. "I only sent the Coast Guard to offer you a few more weeks of your vacation! It's time to come home."

PARODY ON A CHRISTIAN JOKE,
— GARY BURGHOFF, 1992

CHAPTER 16

CR

The sudden frenzy and tension caused by the Chum Magic explosion and eventual, sudden demise had caused new lows of dissention between Elisabeth and me. We had tried to shelter our boys, then three and five years old, from the turmoil, but they had not survived unaffected. It became sadly clear that we, as parents, needed to "make an adjustment." Children are not born to fit into your busy schedule. They are born to receive your undivided attention and love.

I promised Elisabeth that if she would allow me a few weeks of solitude alone in the Connecticut cabin, I would use the time to pray and return a calmer and wiser husband. She agreed to indulge me and as soon as I left, made arrangements to abscond with my precious sons and move to Northern California, where she planned to file for divorce. I learned what had happened upon my arrival in Connecticut when I received the delivery of my sweet housecat "Connecticat," who Elisabeth had hurriedly shipped to me, by airfreight. Though no letter of goodbye had accompanied my furry and frazzled world traveler, the message had arrived, loudly and clearly: *She had stayed with me through THICK.*

I was on my own again, and my boys were Daddyless.

She had deserted the Marathon house, taking her personal savings account and all our personal and financial records with her. For the next few weeks, my Connecticut "recreation" retreat mutated into my gloom and doom room.

It was 1992. Hurricane Andrew thrust his angry fists at Homestead and the Florida Keys with the fury and power of the Hiroshima bomb! Homestead had been leveled and communications with the Keys disrupted. I spearheaded a relief drive among my good, local Connecticut country neighbors, to gather food, clothing and blankets for south Florida's victims and then shot south in my RV toward the Keys.

As I drove through Homestead, which was the last town on the U.S. Continent before entering the narrow road which connected the Keys, I viewed a panorama of total destruction. Of the thousand homes and palm trees I had viewed as I drove to Connecticut a few weeks earlier, not one home, not one palm, remained standing. Continuing to drive south, I held my breath. The Keys' Overseas Highway had become a post-hurricane obstacle course. Key Largo had sustained serious flooding and damage. Islamorada had survived with moderate damage, but was already rebuilding, and by the time I had driven the hundred or so miles and reached Marathon, I was relieved to find our house and property, though a little windblown, otherwise undisturbed.

But it was no longer a home. Without my family, it was a lonely, empty conch shell. And, so again, was I.

As I climbed the stairs of our once-proud family house, I noticed a sole figure at the corner. His respectful dress and modest countenance told me instantly he was a Jehovah's Witness. Before even unlocking the door of the house, I found myself on the corner with him.

"You're a Witness, I take it?" I asked as I approach him.

"I am," he said, modestly, as he transferred his Bible to his left hand, offering me his right. "I'm Brother John Burns."

After inviting him in, we sat in my living room, as I explained the current shambles my life had become. I explained that I was experiencing confusion over finding myself (even after being transformed in the Lord) a total failure at life.

"The Lord had, in His good grace, placed me on the correct and narrow road," I bemoaned. "But I'm even more lost than before."

Brother John smiled (in fact he nearly laughed out loud) as he placed a reassuring hand on my shoulder: "I have no doubt that the road on which you have been undeservedly placed is the Lord's road," he said good naturedly. "But, you have been walking BACKWARDS toward the WORLD, ever since he placed you there!"

I had become, not only lost again, I had wondered so far into the limbo/never-land between Heaven and Earth, that only God Himself could find me. Within an hour, Brother John helped me to unravel my erroneous, spiritual road map.

"Most of the Witnesses" he explained, "are comprised of people just like you, many of them former worldly professionals; doctors, lawyers and even show-business celebrities, who have given up their lofty materialistic ambitions to instead take modest jobs to support their families while joyfully witnessing the Lord's word to those lost in the same spiritual wilderness, where you now find yourself. And there are *millions of us*, who have made that commitment."

My foolish errors became suddenly clearly apparent. Had I not continued my involvement with material gain in my misguided attempt to prove to Elisabeth that I was an "exceptional provider," and had I simply trusted God to lead my way, the simple and harmonious life in Connecticut (which I had instinctively longed for) would have led to the tranquility necessary to hear the Lord whisper His directions toward the modest destiny He had chosen for me.

For the first time, I came face to face with my responsibility concerning my own life.

Satan hadn't even had to turn my head around! It had already, by my own stubborn, worldly nature, ignorance and lack of spiritual knowledge, been facing in the wrong direction. I immediately began attending talks at Marathon's Kingdom Hall.

Sunday School had begun anew.

Now, I won't attempt to coerce you into conversion by listing the pure and simple wisdom I learned from those kind fellow travelers at those Sunday meetings. Their doors are always open to anyone who wishes to walk through them at 10 a.m. on any given Sunday morning and who seeks the same uplifting knowledge. But, I *will* tell you that in two months my mind had been raised with such clarity and my heart reinforced with such renewed spiritual love and security, I was ready to "take care of business" regarding placing the Marathon house up for sale and to make a beeline to California to be with *my boys*! And, this time, I was facing in the Lord's direction!

Westbound Interstate-10, symbolically, was now my road to salvation. Before I left, I picked up a huge pile of mail at my

Marathon post office and at a rest stop, began sorting through it. My BP contract had provided the largest incremental payment in the contract's fifth year. It was year five and the more than fifty commercials I had completed for them were very successful. Their sales were soaring. As I thumbed through the mail, my eyes fell upon a letter from BP's Corporate America office in Ohio. Opening it, (half hoping it included a check) my spirits deflated, realizing it was a termination notice. They had, for whatever reasons, decided not to exercise my final year's option. *I was unemployed.*

I thought of my $7,000 in monthly bills for which I would be responsible. My mother had left me thirty thousand dollars from my parent's estate. It was all the liquid worldly wealth I had left.

Hurricane Andrew's destruction was not only physical, it was psychological. It also demolished the Florida Keys real estate market. I could have to pay the ample mortgage payments on our now deserted Marathon house for years to come.

I phoned Bob Crystal: "Bob? I'm going to have to go back to our theater engagements. Please contact those eleven theaters I made so much money for and start setting up work."

Eight rests stops later, he phoned and responded: "Gary, I'm sorry to report this, but all those theaters have either closed or are no longer able to hire celebrities. The whole theater network has collapsed!"

Thirty thousand dollars divided by seven thousand per month in bills is . . . I had four months and I would be broke. Remembering that God doesn't give you what you want, when you want it, He gives you what you need, when you need it, I pushed on toward Paradise . . . Paradise, California, that is.

Paradise is a little historical mining town, tucked into the mountains, ninety miles north of Sacramento. Elisabeth's mother had retired there after the death of Elisabeth's Father, years before I met her. I had bought a small cabin for us in the neighboring community of Magalia. It was a charmer. Embraced within the oaks and cedars, the little mountain chalet stood on a quarter acre in a subdivision called Paradise Pines. It was a mixed community of doublewide trailers and custom-built homes. Our little all-wood cabin included two small bedrooms, living room, kitchen and single bath downstairs and a spiral staircase, which leads to the roomy upper loft. This is where Elisabeth had brought my sons. I phoned ahead to make her aware that I was on my way and that I intended to find a place of my own. I was determined to share in the raising of our sons, regardless of our divorce. It would mean practically deserting my home in Connecticut and my relationship with my family on the East Coast. My brother Dave and his wife Linda lived only minutes from the Connecticut cottage and (now that our parents had died) we had become closer than ever.

Moving to Northern California would also mean that I would become more isolated from the entertainment industry. In Connecticut, I was only ninety miles from New York City and could easily commute to Broadway job opportunities. Paradise, California was close to nowhere (at least nowhere having anything to do with my career). L.A. is six hundred miles to the south.

But a father belongs with his children, and *this* father intended to love them with every last modicum of his ability, time and commitment!

My son Jordan had been born on December 21, 1988. At my arrival in Paradise he was three months from this fourth birthday. When I drove into the driveway at the cabin, he ran into my arms and whispered, "Daddy, oh Daddy, is your vacation over?"

"I'm here to stay, Jordan. Daddy will never take a *vacation again.*"

Jordan is, even to this day, the best hugger in the world. He doesn't just hug — he holds you close, conveying affection, need, empathy and unconditional love to the hugee. You carry his hugs with you forever.

In the months and years to come, I would become a "Mr. Mom." Elisabeth laid out ground rules, which included that we would not, in any way, try to interfere with each other's personal lives, except concerning our scheduling of separate time with the boys. I assured her that our sons' welfare was my sole reason for relocating. Living by her rules would be a challenge. A father, alienated by separation and divorce in California has unclear and dubious rights. If a disagreement arises between divorced parents concerning their children's welfare, the father is often helpless, under law, to assert his will. I would have to learn to operate in an emasculated fashion, while being "Daddy in Paradise."

But, when you're a *believer*, you rely on God's power, not your own. And He is not a castrated God! Nor is He a chauvinist! If you allow Him, He will lift you up from an oppressive world with dignity and righteous might! I was determined to, while placing my "father's ego" in His hands, let Him do the lifting.

Within a week, I had rented a cozy double-wide, just down the street. Now, as fate would have it, Elisabeth was a "morning person." I, being a theater person and used to working nights, was not. She began working for a local dentist as an assistant, which meant she had an early-to- rise, early-to-bed lifestyle. The fact that I was jobless was, at this time, a blessing. My days were free and my responsibility as a full-time dad was becoming the most rewarding experience of my life.

Miles and Jordan soon moved in with me, into my little three-bedroom mobile home, and "Mr. Mom" was swinging into full action. Though I had always "done my share" during the marriage, regarding caring for the boys, I now was doing it all: the daily laundry, the bathing, food planning and cooking, shopping, moral support, spiritual education, fishing and hiking trips to local streams and lakes, picnics, transportation to and from school, helping with the homework and most of all, on an hourly basis, conveying that I was "glad my sons were born."

My three children, on a moment to moment basis, were continuing to bring a joy into my daily life that my career had never provided.

One day, on our car ride back home from the Catholic school we had enrolled the boys in, Miles was wearing a scowl.

"Miles . . . is something troubling you?" I asked.

"I was just wondering," he plaintively responded. "Is there is, or is there really isn't, a God?"

"*Me, too!*" responded Jordan from the backseat.

I pulled the car over to the side of the rustic, curvy mountain road and safely escorted them both through the local business traffic and into the forest. We hiked far enough into the beautiful woods, so that the traffic sounds would be entirely silenced. We just stood there quietly, for several minutes, until "God's music" began to emerge. A western Blue Jay spoke mournfully. A squirrel chattered from a nearby tree. And a slight breeze rustled leaves all around us. We were surrounded by peace and order.

After enough time had elapsed to acclimate ourselves to the entirely natural surroundings, I asked, in a near whisper, "Can you name anything you see around you that was made by people?"

Their young but curious minds, clicked into gear. "No, except for our clothes," said Jordan. "Then who made all the natural things?" I asked.

The nearby squirrel chattered excitedly, as if attempting to provide his own, very opinionated answer.

Miles said, "It's God, isn't it?"

"That is the question you will one day have to answer for yourself," I responded. "Now is not the time to accept Him into your hearts. Now, when you're young, is the time for you to simply enjoy His creation and give heartfelt thanks that life exists. If you love all the natural things, you will also be loving whoever or whatever made them. And, "whoever" and "whatever" will be loving you back.

Elisabeth and I were becoming aware that Miles, though obviously bright, showed signs of mentally processing information in an unusual manner. On walks through woodsy areas, whenever we encountered mushrooms — many of which were poisonous — we would instruct him: "You see that mushroom? DON'T TOUCH IT." After thoroughly indoctrinating him, one day, upon seeing one on our path, I asked, "Miles, what's that?" Instead of "a mushroom," he responded with *A Touch-it-don't.*

His teachers at school were reporting similar responses. "Miles, how much is eight plus eight?"

"Thirty-two minus sixteen," he would answer.

His teacher suggested that Miles should be tested for Attention Deficit Disorder. Remembering that my mother had A.D.D., I agreed. The test was inconclusive, yet the drug Ritalin was recommended. But Elisabeth and I both agreed that additional love and understanding would yield more valuable results.

In my sometimes-harried parental life, I failed him miserably, now and then: "WHAT'S THE MATTER WITH YOU?" I shouted on more than one occasion, when Miles failed to pay attention to a directive or failed to fulfill the completion of a chore.

"I don't know!" he mournfully responded, his eyes welling up in tears.

What was I thinking? How could I repeat the same destructive, rhetorical question my father had uttered time and time again, which negatively impacted my *own* self-image as a little boy? Here before me was the love of my life and, in my frustration, I was so foolish and weak that I had risked harming him psychologically! Not only was I learning a new empathy for my father's responses to the frustrations of his life when I happened to come along, I was learning that even *I*, who understood how destructive parents can be, was subject to the same pitfalls.

When the smoke cleared after such an outburst, I asked Miles to join me at the dinner table. He was still six years old.

"Miles, Daddy owes you an apology. Sometimes parents say things they regret. I want you take all the times I've said, '*What's the matter with you?*' and flush them down your memory's *toilet*. Instead, I want you to remember that you are, to me, one of the best human beings on earth!"

The grin, which appeared on his suddenly joyful face, made me thankfully aware that I had not been too late in apologizing.

"Dad, you're the best dad in the whole school," he said.

"THAT'S RIGHT!" said Jordan, who had overheard.

"Why?"

"Because you spend more time with us than any of the other daddies — and you teach us," was Jordan's response.

I reflected on the precious blessing the Lord had given me. All my "failure" in life was now being transformed into the *process of succeeding* as a human being. He had imprinted my children with the ability to identify and forgive. A few years later, Miles would be elected "Student of the Month" twice by his fellow seventh-grade students. He earned this title for his "compassion," a category which did not even exist on their selection list, but which they added to express their appreciation of his special nature.

One afternoon a week or so before Christmas of 1994, Miles accompanied me to our quaint Magalia hardware store. I had less than ten dollars in my pocket and sought to buy a light bulb. As we approached the entrance, we paused to admire some edged-glass art pieces being sold by the man who had created them. I assumed he was earning extra money for his own family Christmas expenses. The work was of a high quality and I especially admired a clear circular glass disc mounted on a finely sanded and lacquered stand. The hand-edged scene depicted a hummingbird extracting nectar from a blossom. "This is very beautiful," I said. "How much are you asking?"

"Seventy-five dollars," was his response.

I thanked him politely and, a little embarrassed I couldn't afford the piece, Miles and I entered the store. About ten minutes later, we walked out again, my light bulb bagged and tucked under my arm, and there stood the same kind artisan with the piece I had admired.

"Mr. Burghoff," he said, "I'd like you to have this piece of my artwork to thank you for years of wonderful laughter you have brought my family and me."

I was thunderstruck. I stood there awkwardly, not knowing how to react. After a pause — which threatened to last half the length of this autobiography — my six-year-old Miles said proudly, "Take it, Dad. You deserve it."

At that moment, my world-hardened heart dissolved into complete and humbled gratitude for the life the Lord had given me. He had turned FAME into a conduit of love. People, instead of "jabbing" were suddenly and respectfully offering to share their hearts. And my beautiful son had given me permission to be proud.

A few weeks later, Miles finished reading his first book in his first-grade class. His teacher kept a "treasure chest" in the room from which her students who completed this achievement could choose their reward. Miles, who was born with an eye for beauty, spotted and immediately chose a small crystal glass goose. When his mother arrived to pick him up after school, she recognized Miles' proud reward as an expensive and sought-after collectible, Swedish crystal.

"I'm sorry," she told the teacher. "But I think you've made a mistake. This little glass goose is worth over two hundred dollars. I can't let Miles accept this."

His teacher, who had been divorced, was mortified. She confessed it had been a wedding gift, which her divorce had rendered valueless in her mind, and she had easily included it with the other "treasures."

When I heard about the incident, I immediately called Miles' teacher.

"Do you like wildlife art?" I asked.

"Yes, I do, very much."

I have this little watercolor painting, which I painted. Would you take it for my son's treasure?"

"Oh, Mr. Burghoff, what a wonderful solution! My conscience has bothered me all night and all day today over not being able to give your son his rightly earned reward!"

I brought her my little painting and she gave me the goose. That night when Miles returned from school, I had it wrapped and tied with a ribbon. When he opened it, he read the card, which I had included. It read: "Take it, Miles. You deserve it!"

His precious gift to me had swung full circle, in support of his special and beautiful existence.

و   و   ℘   ℘   و

One night I noticed Jordan (three going on forty), staring apprehensively out the window. I approached him and placed my hand on his little shoulder.

"What do you see out there?" I asked.

"Boy, it's really dark tonight!" he responded.

Remembering my own fear of the dark as a child, I asked, "Would you like to walk outside with me in the dark?"

"Yes, let's do that. I want to see what the dark *really looks like*," he answered.

The narrow circle, which formed our street in front of the trailer, contained only sparsely spaced streetlights. By walking around the curve, we settled at a place which was totally un-illuminated. We silently held hands for awhile until our eyes became acclimated. Suddenly, we became aware that the street and forest trees which lined it were being softly illuminated by the moon and stars above us. Jordan looked up at the sky.

"Daddy, it isn't really dark at all, is it?"

"No, sweetie; God is the creator of light, not darkness. His creation is always illuminated to show its glory, even at night. And, even when we think it's dark, God's light is always shining."

Jordan has never feared the dark.

"HAIR"

I never thought much about hair
I assumed mine would always be there
Then one day I spotted
My scalp was quite dotted
With reflections of skin that was bare

And now, all the hair in my nose
Can be watched, as it rapidly grows
And there's hair in my ears
Which even appears,
To wave in the wind, as it blows

The hair on my head has left home
And gone where the buffalo roam
Though all over my body
I'm furry and shoddy
My head is a Capitol Dome!

Now I'd mention the hair on my —
But it just wouldn't be nice to say what
New growth is descending
(Perhaps I'm offending)
I guess I should keep my mouth shut!

But before this confession is through
There is something I really must do
Without any fear,
I trust you to hear
That the hair on my heart is for you

— EXTENDED LIMERICK BY GARY BURGHOFF
©1996

CHAPTER 17

‫ۿ‬

I was beginning to wonder who that "older person" in the mirror was. When I happened to catch a rerun of *M*A*S*H*, while channel browsing on my television, that Radar fellow seemed only vaguely familiar. I had just turned fifty and though I felt as young as ever, the comb on my sink in the bathroom, was constantly becoming matted with follicles, which had just committed hairy-karri!

Though my life with my boys was fulfilling and active, during the quiet times (especially just before falling asleep at night) the jolting realization that my life was more than half over would render me sleepless.

The Witnesses taught that death was merely a "sleep," which would, in Jehovah's good time be interrupted by the Resurrection. All would be awakened and all would be judged by the condition of their hearts. Those whom the Lord found worthy would resume, forever, on a new paradise Earth.

I found myself wondering if I was ready. What was **my** heart's condition?

For years, I had "sandbagged" resentments toward people in my life who I perceived as having rendered me an injustice. One sleepless night, it occurred to me that I WAS those people. There was not one negative quality which I perceived in any of them, that, if I was honest with myself (and with God), I didn't *also* perceive in my own darkest nature. No wonder I was rapidly aging! The anger and resentment I had harbored for those I thought had done me harm was, in a very real way, *anger toward myself!*

I allowed my active imagination to visualize anger as a demonic assailant within me, choking my heart with hideous and powerful, fleshless fingers!

"Dear Jehovah," I prayed, "in Christ's name, I ask you to bless, with tender graces, all those who have wronged me! I give my anger completely and sincerely over to you. I ask that you substitute, in the spot it has occupied, within my heart, *tolerance and love* . . . especially for Jackie Cooper!"

My hair stopped falling out.

How beautiful we will be
When we realize
How beautiful
We are.

UNTITLED PROVERB BY GARY BURGHOFF,
(NO COPYRIGHT)

CHAPTER 18

CR

In 1993, just after learning that Elisabeth had left me, I took a hiatus from my "pity party" by accepting an invitation from the U. S. Department of the Interior in Washington D.C., to judge the Federal Duck Stamp Competition. The Federal Duck Stamp, for all you non-hunters, is a federal revenue stamp, which each hunter must purchase before every hunting season begins in order to obtain a local hunting license. They are purchased at local post offices. The program, started by President Franklin Roosevelt in 1934, provides federal funds, which the government uses to purchase precious, open wetlands for wild animal sanctuaries. Ninety-eight cents of every dollar raised from the stamp's sales go toward purchasing wetlands.

Bob Lisino, the Program's Director, had learned of one of my post *M*A*S*H* projects, a video called *The Video Guide to Stamp Collecting*, which I had hosted, and in which, I had sung the praises of the Duck Stamp Program.

Over a short four-day period, I found myself, along with four other judges, "locked" in the main viewing hall at the Department of the Interior, completely surrounded by six hundred water fowl paintings, which had been submitted by amateur and professional anonymous painters, who had entered the open national competition.

Four days surrounded by such beauty and the impressive human involvement it took to "create" it, made me wish I could also be a painter. In fact, I couldn't wait to, once the competition was over, get home and set up an art studio! But pending divorce, hurricanes and parental concerns had delayed me.

Now, in 1994, during the quiet times when the boys were at school and in the late evenings after I had tucked them in, the Lord began to whisper *"paint"* . . . *"paint"* . . . *"paint."* I charged $649.97 on my credit card to purchase art materials and set up my easel in my spare bedroom. *"Paint what you know and love."*

I began to paint the environment, not just any environment; the natural world that I had carried around with me in my heart since childhood.

Making numerous trips to California federal and state nature preserves, I gathered candid photographs of animals I had personally encountered throughout my life. The photos would be a reference for the detail my mind and heart had forgotten. But the paintings, I hoped, would share my inner little boy's first discovery of life and the beautiful creatures which had crossed my path. At the very least, I hoped to leave a modest legacy of paintings, depicting my love and respect for nature, to my three children. I had visions of creating a sort of "nature autobiography" on canvas, instead of — well — instead of what you're reading. I guess the Lord has seen fit to bless me with both very joyful experiences.

Anyway, back to the life the Lord has made . . .

I had done some research. Though, there were hundreds of thousands of wildlife art collectors in the United States, they, since the 1970s (when the collector's market hit its peak), had run out of wall space! Accordingly, I decided to paint only small paintings, hoping that the limited edition prints, which I planned to publish from them, would find "welcome corners" on the collectors' otherwise-overcrowded walls.

It was an inspired decision. The small paintings which began to emerge soon struck me as more personal and intimate in nature. I strove to bring the viewer eye to eye with the beautiful other souls which shared our space on the living jewel we call Earth.

I became fascinated with the design on the head of a male wood duck. So, instead of painting the entire duck (as most wildlife artist do), I painted only the head, accenting that beautiful design. When I had finished the eye of the bird reached out to me as a window through which I could glimpse the individual soul contained within. I called my painting, "Eye to Eye." Then I added the Roman numeral "I" to the title because I realized that I could make an even stronger statement by continuing with an entire series of "eye to eye's," each painting connecting the human viewer with the common essence of life and individual personalities which all creatures possess.

"Eye to Eye II" depicted the mournful, questioning gaze of that beautiful and inquisitive red fox I had carried around in my heart since childhood. III was of a bobcat; IV an elf owl and V an American eagle — the fellow fisherman I had always enjoyed and admired. While painting these, I started another series, which I called "The Nesting Suite," depicting mating ducks and geese, involved in the most beautiful phase of their lives: procreation.

Having no training (except for Willard Strassberger's high school art class, thirty-two years earlier) I struggled to create my own technique with each and every (often-disastrous) brush stroke. Willard and another kind art instructor, David Tomori, generously offered to stand by their phones if I needed their assistance in overcoming seemingly unsolvable problems which would, now and then, arise. But, by the time I had called them to explain my confusion, the Lord was already working out the solutions in my mind.

And as I painted, I began to lose my sense of fragmented time — *Man's time*. And I began to experience eternal time — *God's time*.

Though I would set an alarm clock to alert me to stop and pick up the boys at school, prepare dinner and care for them until they were in bed at night, all of the rest of my conscious hours streamed together like an eternal, endlessly flowing river as I joyfully painted the natural history of my heart's life.

In three months' time, I had completed nine paintings. Now the money my mother and father had left me was all but gone. I was facing bankruptcy. I had faithfully made timely payments to all my creditors, but as the sixth-month anniversary since Elisabeth's and my separation rolled in, I had nothing but *eating money* left.

On Sunday morning, I attended the talk at Magalia's Kingdom Hall. As I walked through the door, I was met with the same warmth from my new Witness neighbors that was shown me back in Marathon. When the talk had ended, I asked to speak with an Elder. I explained my financial problem and asked his advice as to how I should proceed. I wanted to avoid filing for bankruptcy protection.

"Your instincts are correct," he said. "Bankruptcy, while legal, is unfair to your creditors. They are our brothers and sisters too, you know."

"Then what should I do?" I asked.

"Call each and every one of them and simply and honestly explain your financial situation. Trust Jehovah to touch their hearts. You may find that your creditors will understand and work with you in rebuilding your financial life. Meanwhile, pray to Jehovah to help you to fulfill your financial obligations."

For a week while the boys were at school, I did nothing but phone my creditors. My humiliation soon turned to gratitude as, as the Elder had predicted, all but one (out of more than twenty) reduced my interest rates, temporarily suspended payments and offered help in advising me in better money management when — and if — I recovered.

IF. An intriguing word. IF, after doing all I could, would the Lord do all the rest? IF I placed my worldly fears — which had plagued me my entire life — aside? IF I learned to abandon worry, would He set things straight for my children and me? Conversely, IF I trusted completely, would my *faith be proven nothing but a foolish and imagined fantasy?*

Now was the best time to find out. I had nowhere to go but up.

"Lord Jehovah, in the name of Christ," I prayed. "I turn all my problems, financial and otherwise, completely and totally over to you! And I give my LIFE to you, also!"

Within weeks, though nearly all *M*A*S*H* residuals had ceased between 1989 and 1994, they suddenly resumed. Art galleries, all over northern California, began to request my work! A new dinner theater in Kansas City, Missouri asked me to reprise *Boney Kern*! Out of nowhere, the Xerox Corporation requested I do a radio commercial campaign for them! ADDI Art Galleries in Reno, Nevada ordered NEARLY ONE THOUSAND PRINTS! I was offered a new PBS television series called *Pets: Part of the Family*, which celebrated the bond we have with our domestic animals. And I won an *Emmy nomination* for *hosting it!* And, Feature Films For Families, an independent motion picture company asked me to create one of the most interesting characters I had ever been offered; Liam Connors in *Behind the Waterfall*. The film also starred nineteen-year-old Gena Gale Burghoff. That's right. My beautiful and *talented* daughter!

And the blessings never stopped!

The Florida Marathon house sold!

"You must have a guardian angel looking over you!" the real estate man had related. "Nothing is selling here right now. Your buyer came out of nowhere and offered top dollar!"

Month by month, year by year, the Lord provided all that was needed to solve my financial woes! Not a penny more, or less.

And I had to do nothing but love Him, and be grateful for His blessings.

He had always been there. Always. In my childhood dream, during family crises, holding me in his arms on the day President Kennedy died, suffering with me on the beach when Jim had ended his life. He brought me Barbara Minkus and Joel Shulman and granted my "big break." He provided familiar and loving companionship during my early days in New York and L.A. He reminded the Preminger brothers and blessed me with "Radar." He had brought me Janet and Gena. He placed me with my creative family on the *M*A*S*H* series. He led me to Elisabeth, Miles and Jordan; protected us from the hurricane and financial disaster, which led me to Paradise and Kingdom Hall.

He had acted in a million ways my human mind could never comprehend or remember. He had been my *underserved mentor.*

Gradually, this realization led me to gratitude, the expression of which took the form of my openness and love for others. Today, though, divorced and living "alone," my simple joy in the Lord has led me to retirement from show business, but full employment with life. My fans have become my friends; and the world . . . my extended family. I reside in Florida in winters, my beloved Connecticut cottage with Miles, Jordan and Gena in summer and fall, and, if He continues to be willing, always with *Jehovah* in the joyful spirit world I refer to as my heart.

Thank you for sharing my life story.

God Bless You.

PHOTOGRAPHS

ⓒⓡ

The Carpenter family. Note Mom (age two) seated on my Great Grandfather's lap; her already developed (and very familiar) scowl proclaiming her dissatisfaction with life.

The Burghoff clan (1911). My Grandparents (far left). Dad is seated on Grandpa's lap.

Mom — her "special celebration of life . . ."

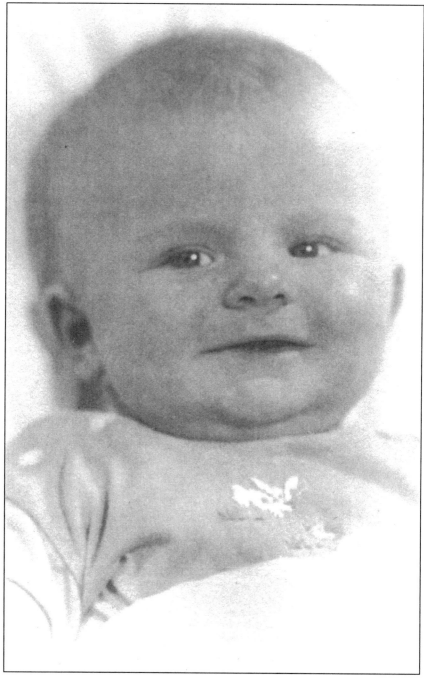

People tell me "babies don't laugh. It's gas." They are wrong. Today I get gas! Back *then* I was born laughing!

My big brother David and me. Florida 1949.

Grams and Gramps, Florida 1949. Mom's mom and my step grandad "Bill."

My father, my brother David and I at home in Forestville, 1950.

Our Christmas mantle, 1950. Note the antique china on the wall.

Mom (a not-so-Merry Christmas).

One of Mom's productions, 1952. She stands next to me (center). I'm wearing my "lonely little petunia" costume with a striped jacket and checkerboard pants. This is from our hometown paper, *The Bristol Press*, published in 2007. They had not forgotten, more than 50 years later. (O.M. stands for "older members.") Bristol Boys Club Benefit, musical producers.

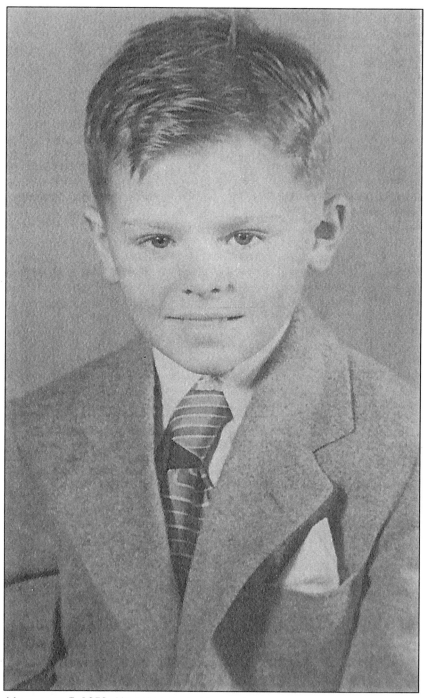

Me — age 7, 1950. Already an aspiring actor.

7th grade class at C.A. Bingham school. I'm 5th from the right — bottom row — age 13.

The Boyfriend, Belfry Theater, Williams Bay, Wisconsin, 1961. I'm on the far left.

My first 8″ x 10″ head shot. (I was 16.)

The original off-Broadway company of *You're a Good Man, Charlie Brown*, 1967. Rear to front: Karen Johnson (Patty), Bob Balaban (Linus), Skip Hinnant (Schroeder), Reva Rose (Lucy), Bill Hinnant (Snoopy), Me (Charlie Brown). Note Reva's expression — I had to face it onstage *and* off!

March 8, 1967 — the opening night party just after reading the rave reviews. Left to right: producer Gene Persson, actress Reva Rose, Me, actress (and wife of Gene Persson) Shirley Knight, producer Arthur Whitelaw.

The *Charlie Brown* company sweater layout for *GQ* magazine, 1967.
Top row, left to right: Bob Balaban (Linus), Bill Hinnnant (Snoopy).
Middle row: Me, Karen Johnson (Patty).
Lower row, Skip Hinnant (Schroeder), and Reva Rose (Lucy).

Janet (of the earth), 1970.

The Gale Family, Malibu, 1970.

Janet and me with Malibu neighbors, Kent and Helen Anderson, in the living room of my little cabin by the sea. This was taken in the early '70's (post-*Charlie Brown*, post-*M*A*S*H* film, pre-*M*A*S*H* television series). It was a poor but happy time for me, when only the Lord provided.

With Janet, 1975 (8 months pregnant).

Janet and me. Photo by good friend Ed Begley, Jr., 1976.

Taking direction from the master, Bob Altman. *M*A*S*H* feature, 1969.

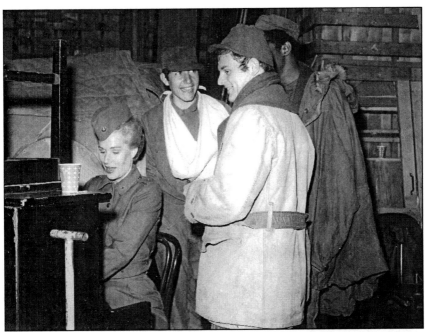

On the set of the M*A*S*H feature — enjoying Sally Kellerman's hot jazz piano playing, 1969.

Three tired actors resting between shots. Don Sutherland, Tom Skerritt and me. M*A*S*H feature, 1969.

With Peter Kastner on the set of *B.S. I Love You*, 1969-70.

I'm not having a stroke! Just imitating a lizard.

Birdman of Malibu

That provocative-sounding title, with no criminal overtones, has become a local beach pseudonym for diminutive Gary Burghoff, the all-knowing, all-seeing Radar of the new M*A*S*H comedy series on CBS (Sundays at 8 PM). Burghoff, an amateur naturalist from early childhood, became interested in rehabilitating ailing sea birds near his beach home after discovering a sick California brown pelican a little more than a year ago. There seemed to be little concern shown by nearby veterinarians over the fate of such unfortunate feathered specimens, prompting Burghoff to take the initiative. He learned from the Long Beach Fish and Game Department that the Los Angeles Zoo and its curator of birds, Frank Todd, would be interested in setting up a treatment center for birds, if he could bring them in.

So for many weeks Gary used an old milk truck as an ambulance and drove the 40 miles from Malibu to the zoo as many as three times a week to supply his feathered patients with vital care. As Burghoff's humanitarian reputation grew locally, he began to receive phone calls from lifeguards, vets and beachgoers who discovered birds encumbered with broken wings and a variety of crippling injuries. It soon became apparent that a nearby treatment center was required to expedite the birds' recuperation, and Burghoff responded to the need by building an aviary in his backyard.

Enlisting the assistance of Malibu veterinarian Dr. Eric Hughes, who set wings, patched up legs and provided other medical aid, the "Birdman" launched his rehabilitation program for pelicans, seagulls, terns, cormorants, Arctic loons and other flying inhabitants of the local environment. Burghoff doesn't represent himself as an ornithologist or a James Audubon, but he admits to having acquired considerable knowledge of bird behavior patterns. "Seagulls have a pecking order," he notes. "When a new bird is added to the aviary, there is a readjustment of the positioning order at feeding time. I have discovered that the best medicine for ailing birds is other birds. They are very competitive about feeding, and it's a healthy thing to have new ones introduced to the pen. This tends to perk up the ailing ones."

Birdman, 1971.

Local Programs Feb. 24-Mar. 2

TV GUIDE

®

15¢ ⊄

Pay Television: The Big Push Is On

Page 5

Cast of 'M*A*S*H'

Our first *M*A*S*H* cast publicity shot for *TV Guide*. First season, 1971.

It takes more than actors to create a hit TV series! The *M*A*S*H* crew, 1974.

Radar & Hawkeye.

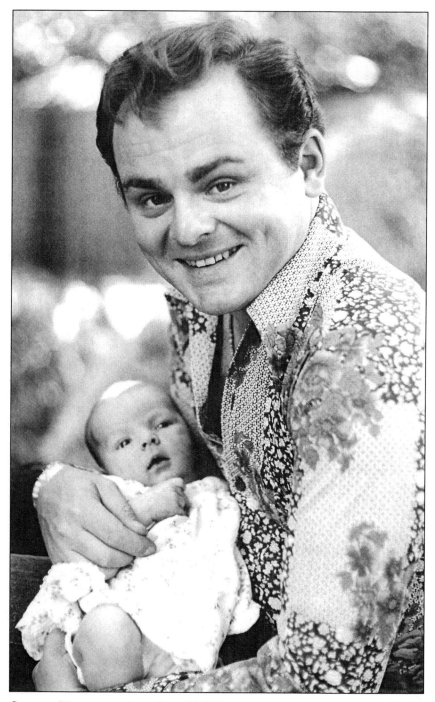

Gena — "the reason I was born," 1975.

A single dad, 1979. With Bridget (left) and Gena (right).

Gena (at the pond).

Jamie Farr and me at a post-*M*A*S*H* reunion in Jamie's hometown, Toledo, Ohio.

Uncle Fran, Aunt Adilade, Gena and me. This was taken shortly after I left *M*A*S*H*. Note the look of "burn out" in my eyes, not to mention the "shield against fame" on my face.

Album cover photo for "Gary Burghoff's (Just for Fun) Dixieland Band,"
New Orleans, 1979-1980.

The Owl and the Pussycat; Earl Holliman's Fiesta Theatre; San Antonio, Texas, 1978.

On the set for a shoot with IBM, with Harry Morgan (who played Colonel Potter on *M*A*S*H*). Harry is one of the finest actors and warmest individuals I've ever known.

The Curved-Butt Spinning Rod and "Chum Magic." The rod is identical to the one I gave the President.

Miles, "pure joy." Florida Keys, 1989.

Proud Miles with an impressive catch. Marathon in the Florida Keys, 1990.

Proud dad, proud son, proud catch! Marathon, 1991.

Jordan — Small Mouth — Big Smile!

April 3, 1991

To Gary —
So many thanks for that special
fishing rod. Great seeing you in the Keys
Geo Bush

President Bush and Quasimodo.

Video jacket cover for *Behind the Waterfall*. Gena is in the lower right

"Home" (the cottage).

The Connecticut cottage. Despite an occasional
bat in the toilet, a retreat to reality.

A proud dad with a beautiful daughter (Gena), Connecticut, 1999.

Cottage (lake view).

Today. A joy to be alive!

ART GALLERY

The artist at work.

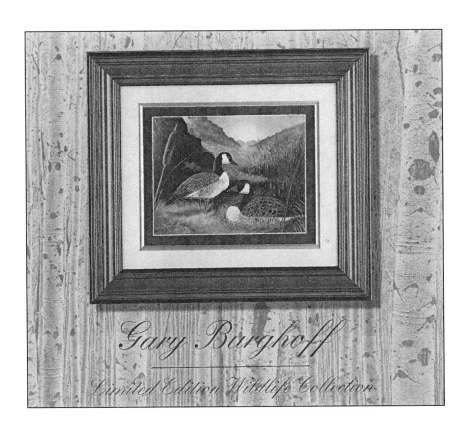

Goldeneye.

Featherbed, 1994.

Daisy Afternoon, 1994.

Spring, 1994.

Dawn of a Generation, 1994.

Turtle Swoop!, 1993.

Eye to Eye I, 1994.

Eye to Eye II, 1994.

Eye to Eye III, 1994.

Eye to Eye IV, 1995.

Eye to Eye V, 1996.

Dawn of a Generation   4 1/2" x 6" Image
Feathered   6" x 4" Image
Eye to Eye 1   4 1/2" x 6" Image
Golden Eye   3 1/2" x 6 1/2" Image
Eye to Eye 3   6 1/2" x 3 1/2" Image
Eye to Eye 2   6" x 9" Image
Turtle Swoop   4" x 5 1/2" Image
Eye to Eye 6   3 1/16" x 7 9/16" Image
Spring   4" x 5 1/2" Image

LaVergne, TN USA
29 March 2010
177402LV00003B/1/P